Freddy:
A Love Story

Ray Oliver

iUniverse, Inc.
Bloomington

Freddy: A Love Story

iUniverse books may be ordered through booksellers or by contacting:

iUniverse
1663 Liberty Drive
Bloomington, IN 47403
www.iuniverse.com
1-800-Authors (1-800-288-4677)

ISBN: 978-1-4620-6430-4 (sc)
ISBN: 978-1-4620-6432-8 (hc)
ISBN: 978-1-4620-6431-1 (e)

Printed in the United States of America

iUniverse rev. date: 11/08/2011

Dedication

To Freddy
And the town that loves him.

Acknowledgements

Writing this book was not my idea. The credit for that goes to a wonderful singer/songwriter/musician – Ryan Long. Ryan is a frequent guest speaker in my creative writing class. After a visit in May 2010, we went to the Apple Blossom Café for lunch. At the conclusion of our meal, I casually commented about a rare occurrence we had shared. I told him that I was surprised that we had finished our lunch and had not seen Freddy.

Ryan is not from Clinton. He did not know to whom I was referring. So I told him a little about Clinton's favorite son. When I finished, he looked across the table and said, "So that's your next book."

I said, "No." I really did not think that I could or should tackle a project of that magnitude. Ryan indicated that he thought it would be a good story to tell, and I agreed. Then he asked, "If you don't tell it, who will?"

That question would continue to replay in my mind until several months later, I found myself beginning what I had initially declined to do. It would prove to be a joyous undertaking. Thanks, Ryan – I won't forget that.

This project would not have happened if the Fagan family wasn't supportive of it. Joe was the only member of Freddy's immediate family I knew before I began writing. Meeting Barbara, Angela, Donna, and John has been a wonderful experience – I am grateful for the opportunity to tell his story.

I would like to thank our hometown newspaper, *The Clinton Courier*

News, for your support, and for allowing me to reprint their article about Freddy and the Christmas money.

Don Calhoun and Alvin Taylor made a huge difference in this book. That is not a surprise – they also made, and continue to make, a huge difference in Freddy's life. It is an honor to be able to call them friends.

Freddy opens doors. Almost every person I approached stopped what he or she was doing in order to help me learn more about Freddy. There are too many to mention here, but you will know who they are by their inclusion in the book. All of your responses are appreciated.

I am grateful to my wonderful colleague, Lisa Harrison Smith, for her support – and for her "help" with the creation of Freddy's Facebook page.

Trying to thank my talented daughter is like trying to describe the Grand Canyon. You just have to experience such awesomeness yourself. Thanks for designing the cover, for the amazing and amusing four hour photo shoot, for creating the blog, and for being you. The girl has the eye of an artist and the heart of an Olympian. Check her work at kbirkbeckphotography.com.

Finally, I want to thank the love of my life. Cindy is my friend, my confidante, my partner in every sense of the word. Thank you for caring and sharing. And typing. I love you.

The Man

He loves Johnny Cash, the Anderson County Fair, and wrestling; a store called Hammers, a restaurant called Apple Blossom, and the Clinton High School Dragons. Especially the Dragons.

For his 50th birthday, the town of Clinton threw a party in his honor and named a street for him. He has been the grand marshal for the annual Christmas parade. He is more popular than any local leader or politician. Almost everyone has a "Freddy story."

He has a football helmet signed by former Tennessee football coach Phillip Fulmer, myriad Hooters girlfriends, and a permanent place in the heart of Colorado Rockies star Todd Helton. He has been mentioned by valedictorians in their commencement addresses. He is a 5'7" whirling dervish of contradictions. He is loud and inappropriate, yet shy and compassionate. He can't subtract or divide numbers, but he can add quality to a person's life. He can't read, but he can educate. In fact, he has taught so many so much for so long that he is the central figure in an ongoing love story.

His full name is Leonard Fredrick Fagan, Jr. It is never used. In fact, he has become an iconic, single-name persona, like Oprah or Madonna. He is a celebrity, a star of the highest magnitude.

To the people of Clinton, and Anderson County, and to those in a surprising number of surrounding communities, he is simply Freddy. This is his story.

Now and Then

The basketball shot is gone now. But for many Clintonians, one of their brightest and fondest memories is of Freddy in the gym -- any gym -- shooting that patented half-court shot of his during halftime, while young kids fought for the rebound and the honor of throwing the ball back to him. The shot was unique, like the shooter himself. It was a combination hook shot/sling shot motion that launched thousands of shots at Clinton Middle School, Clinton High School, and occasional "foreign" gyms.

It was as if a local ordinance decreed that halftime was Freddy time. Occasionally, some youngster would lose his or her head and shoot a rebounded ball. He or she would be admonished, order would be restored, and Freddy would hurl the next shot toward the hoop, and the crowd would wait and hope. When he did make a shot, the eruption that followed was a jubilant, spontaneous celebration worthy of the grandest of achievements. Freddy would laugh, and bow, and point, and high five, and laugh some more.

There are different halftime shows now, but none more poignant.

The signs of aging are obvious. They begin with his hair, that great mane that has gone from brown, to golden, to… well… pick a color. It is gray now, as is his beard -- when he has a beard. There are lines and wrinkles also, especially around those magical windows to his soul – his eyes. The wrinkles and lines help define his face, but his heart remains ageless.

He walks slower. A broken hip from a 2008 Christmas Eve fall will do that to a person. He always had a distinct walk -- a shuffle really. His left arm never leaves his side. His left leg tends to lag behind, constantly playing catch-up, but for years he reached remarkable speeds. He ambles now, more cautious in his movements. But he still roams the streets of Clinton.

Freddy was born on May 30, 1956 -- Memorial Day. Somehow, that seems appropriate. That holiday is now celebrated on the final Monday of the month. His birthday celebration is also flexible, lasting for days and even weeks. Somehow, that seems appropriate, too.

He was born in Germany, at Bitburg Air Base. His now deceased father, Leonard, Sr. was stationed at nearby Hahn Air Force base, but Bitburg had the natal care facility. Immediately, he had trouble breathing. His mother, Barbara, sensed that the doctors feared he might die, although no one voiced those concerns to her. He was initially fed with an eyedropper, remaining in the hospital for about one week.

What followed the hospital stay was three years of change and uncertainty. There was projectile vomiting caused by a reaction to various formulae (whole milk solved the problem). There was a move to France, and then Albuquerque, New Mexico, and then Smyrna, Tennessee. Barbara sensed something was wrong, but had no way of knowing for sure. The medical community was not particularly forthcoming or considerate. A doctor in Albuquerque casually remarked, "He'll never be a PhD." That was as close to a diagnosis as Barbara would receive.

Two specific events would provide the missing information. The first would be the birth of Joe Fagan. Joe was born thirteen and a half months after Freddy. It was as if Joe would provide the developmental model Freddy was lacking. Freddy didn't really stand until Joe did. He didn't walk until his younger brother did, and while this was positive in many ways, it made clear the fact that Freddy was, developmentally, behind.

After seeing the stark evidence, it was obvious that something needed to be done. The second event occurred at Vanderbilt Children's

Hospital. The results would be four words -- four words that would shed the first light into Freddy's behavior.

The first two words would be cerebral palsy. On their website, the National Institute of Neurological Disorders and Stroke defines cerebral palsy as, "Any one of a number of disorders that appear in infancy or early childhood and permanently affect body movement and muscle coordination, but don't worsen over time." It is caused by abnormalities in the part of the brain that controls muscle movements. It is common for it to affect only one side of a person. In Freddy's case, it is the left side. That is why his left arm and left leg are so weakened.

The other two words were also harsh. They were, in the vernacular of the day, mentally retarded. Those four words might devastate some, but for Barbara Fagan, it did the opposite. When asked for her reaction to the diagnosis, her answer is, "Relief. I was relieved because, for the first time, I knew what I was dealing with."

Such a reaction is extraordinary, but not surprising -- at least not after one gets to know the family. It is the first of numerous extraordinary reactions, proving that words and labels cannot define or limit an individual or a family. That's part of the beauty of the story.

Seen Around Town

In her classic novel *Ethan Frome*, Edith Wharton introduces the reader to the title character with these words: "If you know Starkfield, Massachusetts, you know the post office. If you know the post office you must have seen Ethan Frome drive up to it... and you must have asked who he was."

Ask any Clinton High School student to make modern day equivalents for the town of Clinton and the responses are telling. The site may vary. Instead of the post office, students may suggest Hammers Department Store, or Hoskins Drug Store, or the Apple Blossom Cafe, or the Ritz Theatre. They may even suggest the football field. But while the site may vary, the person never does. It is universally accepted that Freddy is Clinton's well-known character.

It begs the question: Why is Freddy so popular? Other towns have people who face similar physical and mental challenges. In fact, Freddy is not the only person in his community with these issues. But no one seems to be as well known or as well loved. What makes him so unique?

Perhaps Melanie Walker Robinson said it best. "I don't have a lot of positive memories from my childhood or living in Clinton, but hearing Freddy's name brings positive memories and puts a smile on my face." Melanie is one of the main reasons that Clinton High School has a dance team. Of course, if C.H.S. has a team, Freddy will be involved. Melanie recalls the 1994 – 96 school years.

"We danced with the band, and everyone knew he was the drum major. He also wanted to be a Dancin' Dragon." Images of Freddy leading the band are vivid in the minds of everyone who has attended a football game. Picturing him dancing with the all girls team is a richly rewarding exercise.

So what makes Freddy special? It is his personality, his ability to touch people permanently. He is not afraid to try new things, such as leading the band or dancing with the dance team. Perhaps he is as uninhibited as everyone else would like to be. Melanie has not been a Dancin' Dragon for 14 years, but she smiles at the thought of Dancing Freddy. She adds, "I put it like this. It was never a question of what was wrong with Freddy, because there were so many things right about him."

Fourteen years later, things have come full circle for the dancers. Freddy loves another one-name icon – Elvis. He loves to imitate him, so much so that he has done it at various public events. He has the costume and the moves. He was scheduled to reprise his Elvis act as part of a basketball half time show with the Dancin' Dragons. Then he fell and broke his hip. When he had recovered, the dance team danced, two lines were formed, and "Elvis" was wheeled into the gym as Clinton High School athletic director Jim Davis proclaimed, "Freddy is the king – the King of Clinton." There were few dry eyes when it happened.

Melanie uses the past tense when she discusses Freddy. Not much has changed, although some of the energy has, in fact, waned. That is to be expected. But the legacy will not change. The manner in which he touched the heart of Melanie Walker Robinson is an often repeated theme. He is an inspirational person. There is a great deal to be learned from someone like Freddy. It only requires a little time, a little effort, and a willingness to listen. It is amazing how many have done so. Long live The King.

Fredcabulary

To someone meeting Freddy for the first time, it is not always easy to understand what he is saying. His speech isn't always clear, and his speech patterns are... well... his.

Many of the nuances will be detailed in later chapters, but a few introductory pronunciation guides are offered here -- sort of a Freddy-speak primer. The first fascinating idiosyncrasy is the manner in which Freddy refers to himself. The word "I" does exist. The contraction "I'm" does not. Sometimes he uses "me" instead of "I." The word that most often follows "I" or "me" is the word "mad." "Me mad" is a common conversation starter. Reasons for the madness are varied, but being mad seems to make Freddy happy.

Sometimes, there is more than a single "me" to start a conversation. Extreme happiness or anger can, occasionally, be measured by the number of times the word is used. "Me, me, me fair 'morrow" translates into, "I am going to the Anderson County Fair tomorrow and I couldn't be more excited."

Actually, the word "morrow" in the above example isn't exactly correct. Tomorrow morphs into a one syllable word. The initial "t" and "o" disappear. The final "o" and "w" do as well. The word becomes "marr" or "marrah."

He does a unique thing if he wants to include someone else in a future trip to the fair, as in, "Who is going to the fair?"

His answer will be, "Me, you, everybody." It's a Fredformula: Two people + one other possibility = the entire known world. What makes the formula so rich is that he often points to the other person when he says "me" and to himself when he says "you." Attempting to explain the pronunciation of the word "everybody" is like trying to balance a chemical equation. Suffice it to say that it is about two and a half syllables, and the letters "v" "y" and "d" are, at best, optional.

"Stink" is an often used word, especially related to sports teams. Stink is pronounced "tink."

Anderson County High School is known as the Mavericks. Fortunately, Freddy has never tried to say the word Maverick. They are, in Freddy World, the Bulls. And he will not hesitate to tell people, "Bulls tink."

And then there are the Oak Ridge Wildcats. They tink, too. Only they have morphed from Wildcats to Pussycats. Sometimes it is pronounced Pushycats.

One of Freddy's favorite places is the Apple Blossom Cafe -- known exclusively as Jane's. Jane Treece is the manager, and Jane's is where Freddy eats many free meals. "Jane" is one of the few names he says correctly.

Syntax takes a beating, especially when Freddy wants to express a negative. If he is not going to go somewhere, he says, "Me go no." If someone hasn't given him a present he says, "Me present no." That specific unpardonable sin, i.e. the present presentation failure, will be addressed in greater detail later.

One of the more unique Freddyisms is the word "shatting," or more correctly, "shattin'." People seem to do a lot of "shattin' 'round" in Clinton. It is not clear where the word comes from. It may be a variation of the old phrase, "Cattin' around." Or it may be: shat tin (verb) Colloquial Freddyspeak -- The act of being idle or uninvolved; loafing. Example -- John was just shattin' 'round, not doing much of anything.

A fancy car is called a cool cat car. Any C.H.S. team is known as, "My boys." During basketball season Freddy gets excited about, "Boy game /Girl game. "

It seems difficult, if not impossible, for Freddy to answer a question with a simple yes or no. "Shoot yeah" is often used -- only shoot may be drawn out for at least five seconds. Other words that may precede yes or no include, but are not limited to, numerous cuss words (some invoking God) in myriad combinations.

"You me pals" is a fine compliment. And, to show his incredibly sensitive side, his use of the word "shame" is always appropriate and touching. Any misfortune, including death, is met with a most sincere, "Shame."

Police officers are, "One Bullet Barneys," a surprisingly clever reference to Barney Fife. However, there was an extended period of time when Freddy patrolled Clinton wearing a badge while carrying a whistle and handcuffs. A plastic gun completed the outfit. Occasionally, the tables were turned and Sheriff Fagan was called "One Bullet Barney." This might cause Freddy to use his special communication skills. He might cuss, he might say, "Me One Bullet Barney, no—You Barney," or he might simply change the subject. When Freddy does not wish to discuss something, no one is better at changing the subject. If he does not like the way a conversation is going, he just starts talking about something else, and repeated attempts to return to the forbidden subject are usually futile.

When Freddy has money, and he often does, he exclaims, "Me rich." The word rich may be multi-syllabic, and various vowel sounds may occur before the final "ch." The green stuff that makes Freddy rich is pronounced "nunny."

Freddy's love of sports is legendary. He loves to stand behind the backstop and yell, "Strike" before the pitch gets halfway to home plate. If the umpire does not agree, boos are heard. The ump, sometimes called ref, may in fact be told, "He tinks." His ability to officiate baseball is not limited to balls and strikes; he also umpires the bases. "You out" is yelled, accompanied by the proper hand gesture. It is amazing how those two words and that one gesture can be applied to non-athletic events.

People who anger Freddy have a special name -- Dumb Dumb. A person can become a Dumb Dumb by:

1. Rooting for the Bulls

2. Rooting for the Pushycats

3. Disagreeing with Freddie

4. Dating one of Freddy's many girlfriends.

Any of those offenses may result in the offender being told, "You out." The reason for item number four being included is that most females in Clinton who spend any time with Freddy will, eventually, become his girlfriend. And if there is any word in Freddyspeak that deserves its own chapter, girlfriend is that word.

The Ladies Man

One of the most significant words in Freddy's life is the word girlfriend. In fact, Freddy's list of girlfriends is larger than most phone directories – an ever expanding collection of his chosen ones. It is the word itself that amuses.

Hearing Freddy pronounce the word girlfriend is one of life's simple pleasures. Usually, the word is accented on the second syllable -- and his voice rises slightly as if he is asking the question. The letter "l" disappears, replaced by an additional "r." Phonetically, it appears as, "gurr FREND?" The final "d" is optional. Sometimes the end sound is dragged out. So a woman could be his "gurr FREENN(D)?" The Southern accent adds the perfect spice to the word. No matter how he says it, Freddy has girlfriends. Good-natured arguments have been known to take place as friends argue over who is the favorite "gurr FREENN(D)" And males who have the audacity to talk with, date, or marry one of Freddy's chosen are in for some serious verbal abuse. They will be told to go. They will be dismissed the same way opposing players are belittled at Dragon baseball games, with the words, "You out!" Just as Freddy rarely uses the word "I'm," he does not often use the word "you're."

Sometimes, depending on the excitability factor, he uses the word "me "more than once. For example, if he is particularly disturbed about a male encroaching on his chosen female, he may say, "Me, me, me mad. You gurr FREENN(D) no. You out. My girl."

Sometimes Freddy raises his fist. It is his initial, non-verbal response to those evil males who may encroach on his territory; his way of suggesting he might have to give someone a knuckle sandwich – not that he would.

Abbey Taylor Harris knows the drill. She was a self-described baseball groupie in high school. She says, "As I attended more and more of the baseball games, Freddy and I became better friends. One day he walked over and gave me a picture of him, as if to say, 'If you are going to be my girlfriend, you have to carry a picture of me in your wallet.'"

Of course Abbey did exactly that. A decade later, she still has it. After giving the picture to her, Freddy told her boyfriend, "She my gurr FREENN now. Shoo boy." He would actually boo his "rival" -- rooting for him to strike out.

Every game, Freddy asked to see his picture. Abbey would show it to him and he would laugh (and occasionally blush). Then the inevitable happened -- their first "fight" as boyfriend and girlfriend. It began with the words, "Me mad." It ended with, "Me picture no." Freddy was upset that Abbey hadn't returned the favor by giving him a picture of her. This became a recurring theme at every ball game.

Abbey adds, "After genuinely being affected by Freddy being mad at me at every baseball game, I gave him one of my school pictures. I said, 'Okay boyfriend, put it in your wallet.' He said he would, and put it in his pocket. The next game I said, 'Hey boyfriend, where's my picture?' He said, 'In your wallet,' thinking I was referring to the picture he had given me. I said, 'No, where is the picture of me that I gave you?' He said, 'Me wallet no. Too many gurr FREENS.' Too funny." Freddy was just being truthful – he had too many girlfriends to keep their pictures. But woe to the girl who didn't keep his and produce it on demand.

To this day, Abbey reacts with the joy and humor typical of those who have had a close encounter with Freddy. She knows that he is right -- he really does have too many girlfriends. Not that he won't find more.

Sometimes his approach is less subtle. Lisa Harrison Smith currently teaches at her alma mater. She recalls being at a C.H.S. basketball game during her high school days when Freddy walked up to her, declared that she was his girlfriend, and placed her wrist in a handcuff. He then placed his own wrist in the other cuff. For half an hour they were linked together. Freddy said that he didn't have the key, which he did, and eventually used it to free Lisa, but not before repeatedly pointing to his cheek and asking for a kiss in exchange for her freedom. It is indicative of the fact that Freddy has a sense of humor and likes to tease people.

Freddy's love of keys and police paraphernalia will play a large role in later chapters. For now, the focus is on the ladies man, who usually finds his girlfriends in a less dramatic manner.

Brittany Jackson is a very attractive former member of the Lady Vols basketball team. She is a statuesque blonde who has dabbled in modeling. Twice she has entered the Clinton High School gym. Twice she has experienced the charm of Freddy.

On one occasion, she was the color analyst for local station broadcasting a C.H.S. basketball game. During the broadcast, Freddy's eyes remained fixed on her. He let it be known that he wanted her autograph. With the help of his pal Alvin Taylor, he eventually secured that prize. When he received it, he quickly and repeatedly tapped his heart, as if being in her presence caused palpitations. What is interesting about his approach is the effort it required. Freddy had to climb the bleacher stairs to get the autograph. Freddy has great difficulty climbing stairs and usually avoids doing so. Apparently, Brittany was worth the climb.

Brittany's second appearance at the C.H.S. gym was to watch her sister play against the Dragons. Brittany's entrance literally created a commotion. She entered, sat down, and immediately found herself sitting next to her new boyfriend. He remained with her for the entire game. Typically, she was gracious and kind to Freddy. Most people are. He has the ability to bring out the kindness in others, especially his girlfriends.

Ashley Duncan knows. As another member of the Freddy Fagan Girlfriend Association, she says, "What's funny is that when Freddy first began calling me his girlfriend, I thought I was the only one. Well, I quickly learned that he sure had me fooled. But I am still honored to be on Freddy's long list of girlfriends."

Ashley's use of the word "honored" is telling. It is telling because in other situations, it might be considered embarrassing, or scary, or any number of potentially negative things. But in Clinton, Tennessee it is an honor to be one of Freddy's girls. How's that for insight into the character of a community?

Clinton

The City of Clinton website offers the perfect sketch of the county seat for Anderson County. It was founded in 1801 and called Burrville, in honor of Vice-President Aaron Burr. Then Burr shot and killed Alexander Hamilton, and the name was changed to Clinton. The website acknowledges that it is possible the town was named for DeWitt Clinton, but concludes it is far more likely it was named after Vice-President George Clinton, who succeeded Burr as Thomas Jefferson's V.P., and also served with James Madison.

While Clinton is a town of under 10,000, Anderson County's website shows over 70,000 residents. It is proud of its Appalachian heritage. It is an area greatly influenced by the TVA and the creation of Norris Lake. The neighboring city of Oak Ridge played a major role in the Manhattan Project – the secret project that created the atomic bombs that were dropped on Hiroshima and Nagasaki.

Recently, Clinton celebrated the 50th anniversary of one of the most significant events in Tennessee history. The Green McAdoo Cultural Center describes it this way: "On August 27, 1956, twelve young people in Clinton, Tennessee walked into history and changed the world. They were the first students to desegregate a state-supported high school in the South. Clinton High School holds the honor of having the first Black to graduate from a public school in the South."

Keith MacDaniel's extraordinary documentary, *The Clinton 12*, chronicles the controversy and anger that resulted from the desegregation – a story that includes the high school being blown up. The twelve individuals were spit on, called names and faced threats and intimidation. Clinton, like much of the country, would have to assess its treatment of people who were "different." Some would react negatively, even violently. Others would react with courage and compassion. Acts of kindness and acts of malice were plentiful.

Most Clintonians know the brief history described here. The question is, "What does all of this have to do with Freddy Fagan?"

Freddy was three months old when Clinton High School was integrated. When he began school, the educational philosophy of the time was not the inclusive one prevalent today. Special education students were also victims of prejudice. Taunts and cruelty and physical violence were possible to anyone who was different, whether the difference was because of a skin color, a physical problem, or a mental challenge.

In 2007, the surviving members of the Clinton 12 received a standing ovation on the football field they once could not walk on. It would be easy to view that incredible, demonstrable sign of progress and forget the difficulty required to get there.

Likewise, it is easy to view the beautiful, compassionate concern Freddy receives now and assume it was always that way. That would not be correct. Special education students have had their own obstacles to overcome. Freddy has been ridiculed, beaten, and berated. There are those who do not wish to associate with special needs human beings. Today, Freddy would be mainstreamed in Anderson County's public schools. Back then, he was segregated to Daniel Arthur – a facility no longer operating. The two stories parallel each other.

The road to equality for minority students, and the road to acceptance for special education students has not been easy. Both were made more difficult by those who would harbor or condone prejudice. But in both cases, the basic goodness of the people of Clinton would triumph. It is a triumph for which Clinton can be proud.

Barbara

"I always thought that Freddy's life would make a good story, I even thought of writing it myself, but I wasn't sure how." Motherly pride exudes from Barbara Fagan when she talks about her oldest son.

She is quiet, reserved. She speaks in simple terms about Freddy, even as she recognizes the complexities of the topic. "He was just one of the family" sums up her child-rearing philosophy.

Barbara Noe was born in Pikeville, Kentucky. Her parents moved to Oak Ridge in the 40's to work in the plants. They were part of the Manhattan Project. She went to Oak Ridge High School, but her parents moved to Mobile, Alabama during her junior year. Barbara stayed in Oak Ridge to finish that year, and then joined her parents. She had met Leonard Frederick Fagan through a mutual friend. Her future husband, who was three years older, joined the Air Force, and after she moved to Mobile, she thought they would not see each other again. When he ended up stationed not far from her home, they began to date.

Barbara was married by the age of 18; she had her first child, Freddy, at the age of 19. Then came Joe, followed by Angela, Donna, and finally John. In fact, the Fagan children have an interesting history when it comes to their birthplaces. Freddy was born in 1956 – in Germany. Joe was born in 1957 – in France. Angela was born in 1959 – in New Mexico. Donna was born in 1962 – in Tennessee. Fifteen years after Freddy's birth, John would join the family. He was also born in Tennessee. Five children -- and only two were born in the same state.

It is important to remember that Freddy's formative years were during the late 50's. Society's understanding of and reaction to special needs children was far different than it is today. Often, those individuals were isolated. There were stigmas attached to them. It was easy to search for a person to blame – as if someone had done something to cause the physical and/or mental challenge to occur. Like all other forms of prejudice, fear and ignorance prevailed – and fathers were not immune from such destructive forces.

The Fagan's marriage would last for 22 years. Those in the immediate family seem to agree that Freddy, Sr. was a bright man, a talented man, a man with a remarkable sense of humor. They also agree that alcohol changed all that; that he could be cruel, especially to Freddy, once he was under its control. It seems he struggled with the reality of having a special needs son. He struggled not because of any additional hardships caused by his presence, but because of the blow it was to his sense of fairness. How could he, a bright man, have a child like that?

His brother Joe recalls how, when his father's drinking was at its worst, Freddy would warn his brother. They shared a bedroom, and Freddy learned to say, "Sshh – Daddy's home."

Freddy was hurt by his father's reaction and treatment, and he was hurt by his father's leaving. In 1977, Mr. Fagan moved to Florida.

The Fagans always allowed their children a great deal of freedom. In Freddy's case, it might not have mattered. He was not about to be confined. He was restless, headstrong, and curious. That would prove to be a difficult combination. Freddy roamed the streets of Clinton, starting at an early age. He walked. Later, he would ride a bike. He seemed to always be on the streets.

Barbara has heard the criticism. She has heard people say, "It's just not right. That boy should be home – he should not be allowed to roam." Once she was watching a baseball game on a frigid afternoon. Freddy came by wearing a short sleeve shirt. The woman sitting next to her -- clearly unaware of Barbara's identity -- tsked her disgust. "Look at that – how can they let him run around with no coat on." Barbara responded, "I tried -- he just won't wear it."

She's heard worse. She has heard adults say, "People like him should be institutionalized. They shouldn't be part of our society." She has heard speculation about how dangerous he might be. She has seen parents not allow their children to play with him.

Fortunately, that was a long time ago. No one talks about institutionalizing him now – they speak about how he has become an institution.

Barbara seems at peace with the way her life has gone. After years of working as an operator for the phone company, she retired and began providing childcare for two families, and basking in the glow of her five children and six grandchildren. She retired again, this time from the childcare business for others. Now, she cares for one child – her first great granddaughter.

Barbara Fagan has persevered. She has maintained an optimistic outlook and a sense of humor. Mention her oldest son and her face lights up. She knows how special he is. She also knows how special Clinton is. She wants her community to know that she is grateful – grateful for the help, for the encouragement, for the thousands of kind gestures that have made all the difference to her family. She was the first to offer this loving testament to her hometown: "In many other communities, Freddy does not survive."

The Mayor

"Everyone knows Freddy is really the mayor of Clinton. I just happened to get elected." With those words, Clinton Mayor Scott Burton identifies the symbolic reality of Clinton's power structure. Scott may have won his campaign, and he may have the title, but Freddy long ago won the hearts and minds of the people of Clinton.

Mr. Burton became the mayor in 2010, and Freddy may have helped. It is a classic story that combines Freddy's love of shirts with his love of money.

Like so many Freddy stories, it began at a Dragon football game. Mr. Burton was actively seeking Mr. Fagan. He had a business/campaign proposition to offer. When he found Freddy, he proposed a deal. If Freddy would wear the "Scott Burton for Mayor" campaign shirt, he would give Freddy twenty dollars. Freddy quickly agreed and donned the shirt.

That seemingly simple transaction may, in fact, speak volumes about Freddy's stature in his community. It says that a candidate for political office is willing to pay for Freddy's "endorsement" – that having him wear a campaign shirt is a good political strategy.

The story does not end there. As is often the case in business transactions, the two sides had a different understanding of the terms of the agreement. Mr. Burton thought he was paying a one-time fee for the service being provided. Mr. Fagan construed the fee to be twenty dollars <u>per game</u>. That became evident when, at the next home football game, Freddy was searching for Mr. Burton with shirt on and hand out. It should be obvious who prevailed in that disagreement. A mayoral candidate stands no chance against an established icon.

The mayor laughs about it, saying, "It was worth it. He probably got me votes. He'd see people, point at the shirt, and tell them to vote."

While the campaign story is humorous, the mayor's view of Freddy's importance to Clinton is not a laughing matter. He is nine years younger than Freddy, so he is correct when he says, "I don't know Clinton without Freddy." As someone who was, as they say in the South, "Born and bred" in the city he now runs, the pride he feels is obvious when he adds, "We've gotten more out of him than we have given to him. He has made us more caring and loving."

Scott fondly recalls growing up in a simpler time – a time with a much different downtown. The center of the action was near Market Street. His mom, Peggy, worked at the Union Planters Bank that has since relocated. Freddy would visit, and he would visit Twins' Café, a landmark that no longer exists. Scott's brother Barry is close in age to Freddy's sister Donna; his sister Laura is close in age to Freddy's sister Angela, so the two families know each other well. Because of that, Scott has always felt a special bond with the Fagans.

He recalls a time when Richard Little got Freddy to take a cluster of Union Planters' balloons to the rival Third National Bank. When Freddy returned, the only word he would say was, "Out." Then he would point, allowing all to know how the prank was greeted by the competing bank.

How does Freddy refer to the mayor? With one word: "Boy." Who else could call a local leader "boy" and do so without being considered rude or offensive? In Clinton, the response to such behavior would be, "That's just Freddy."

Freddy remains nonchalant about the entire situation. Being the mayor really isn't that big of a deal – at least not after being dubbed King.

The Mayor – Part II

Scott Burton's declaration of Freddy as the Mayor of Clinton is not the first time he has been given that title. Clinton Middle School science teacher Mike Graham tells an amusing "mayoral" story:

"Back in the early 90's, I was the head basketball coach at Clinton Middle School. Freddy would come by practice, and would always ask when the next ball game was going to be. We played an early season tournament in Rockwood, and I told Freddy when the bus would be leaving. Sure enough, Freddy was right on time so we loaded up and hit the road.

"When we came into the gym, a pretty stern-looking man was at the ticket gate, and he was making sure that the school was not going to miss out on one dollar of gate money. As we walked by the ticket desk, I had to identify each of my boys as a player, a statistician, a manager, and even had to assure the guy that my assistant coach was actually a coach. And then there's Freddy.

"When Freddy walked up to the ticket table, he looked at the guy and in true Freddy style said, 'Boys . . . ball game.' The ticket guy looked at me kind of puzzled and said, 'And who is he?' I replied, 'This is the mayor of Clinton.' Freddy grinned that typical Freddy grin, raised his head high like royalty and casually strolled into the gym. The next night when we went back, Freddy was there with his Clinton Middle School basketball jersey on that I had given him. (I coached several different sports over the years, and I always knew Freddy would be expecting a shirt, but he seemed to like the jerseys better. In fact, it's hard

to determine if Freddy has more jerseys or girlfriends, but that's a whole 'nuther story' as my grandmother would say).

"Anyway, the following night when we came back to Rockwood for a late night game in the winner's bracket, the same fellow was at the ticket counter, but this time he had a helper, and a policeman was standing by the table. As the team had all passed the ticket table, all three of the men at the table looked at Freddy and the guy from the night before said, 'He's okay, he's the mayor of Clinton,' to which Freddy replied, 'Me Coach!'"

It is sometimes fun to speculate on the conversations that must take place after the Fagan Express has passed through, leaving befuddled bystanders in his wake.

Joe

"He ain't heavy, he's my brother." With those words, Joe Fagan concisely depicts his philosophy about his older brother. The words could not be more appropriate.

In 1917, Catholic priest Father Edward Flanagan founded Boys Town in Omaha, Nebraska. It was a place for neglected and orphaned boys. He would be the inspiration for a 1938 movie, and he would eventually see a drawing of an older brother carrying a younger one. The words Joe so appropriately quotes were under the picture. That picture would inspire a statue at Boys Town, and those words would become their official motto. And even though Joe is the younger brother chronologically, he acts very much as the protective older brother, sometimes figuratively carrying his brother.

In 1969, the British rock band The Hollies used the Boys Town's motto to create a hit song. Clearly, it is a song that touches Joe's heart, but it might be the theme song for the manner in which the town of Clinton embraces Freddy.

Joe's earliest and fondest memories include holding hands with Freddy, Angela, and Donna, as the four of them walked to church. He smiles at the thought of his older brother's love of The Duke – John Wayne. He reveals that Freddy is a "pack rat" who keeps everything. He points out that their mom has a storage unit, full of Freddy's "stuff," including many unopened gifts.

He recalls Freddy playing with the neighborhood kids, just

being part of the group. There were some things he couldn't do, but there were many that he could. He was a master at rolly bats, where the object was to roll a baseball and hit a bat that was lying on the ground. His aim was surprisingly good. When Freddy learned how to skip rocks at the lake, his aim was remarkably bad. He hit Joe in the back of the head with an errant throw.

He remembers camping trips and fishing trips at Point 19 on Norris Lake. He remembers their father telling Freddy that he had to sit very quietly and watch his float if he wanted to catch fish. Somehow, the boy who loved to wander the streets of Clinton was able to sit for hours, calmly fishing. He still can. He still loves to fish.

Joe remembers the pool halls, and the wrestling matches, and as he grew older, the increased responsibility. Never once did it seem like a burden, in fact, quite the opposite. The proof is seen in one simple sentence: "I used to take Freddy with me on my dates." Where other high school students might have been self-conscious, even embarrassed, Joe clearly was not. One can only imagine the reaction of the dates who had not one, but two Fagan escorts. It is possible that Freddy's love of sports is at least partially related to the fact that Joe was very interested in athletics growing up.

It was Joe who had the unenviable task of trying to convince Freddy that his "nunny" should be in the bank. This occurred when he discovered his brother had two wallets full of money – about $900 worth. Freddy's response was, "My nunny." Eventually, Joe prevailed.

Joe married his wife in 1980. After their two children, Katie and Murray, became adults, Joe and Meggie moved to Florida, and while the distance is sometimes hard on them, they manage to talk every day. Joe observes, "I love my family. I love my wife and children. I love my mom and my brothers and sisters. But Freddy is my best friend."

Why wouldn't he be? They are only thirteen and a half months apart in age. They share a name and a love of sports and a pride in each other. Joe calls Freddy, "My pride and joy." Many Clintonians would agree. He certainly is not heavy – and he certainly is everyone's brother.

What's In a Name?

Freddy cusses. Often. And while some of his words may be difficult to fathom, his cuss words are clearly enunciated and easily understood.

His favorite cuss word is damn, although he is not afraid to use the others. Freddy cusses when he is happy. He also cusses when he is mad, and he is often mad. "I mad," or "Me mad" is frequently his attempt at starting a conversation, followed by the reason for his anger. Any slight will do – not taking him with you on your vacation, not giving him a shirt, not naming your first born child after him, just about any offense will suffice.

But there is one unpardonable sin – a sin that will confine a person to the Fagan doghouse for eternity – or until money changes hands. That sin is failure to provide Freddy with a birthday present.

There is a group of people who, because of their close relationship with Freddy, or past practice, or some pre-ordained cosmic destiny, MUST provide the birthday boy with a present. PROMPTLY. Failure to do so may cause the word damn to replace your first name. A typical conversation between the birthday boy (B.B.) and John Q. Public (J.Q.P.) might be:

B.B.: I mad.
J.Q.P: You're mad?
B.B.: Shoot yeah. I mad Damn Gene.

J.Q.P: Why are you mad at Gene?

B.B.: Me present no.

J.Q.P: Gene didn't get you a present?

B.B.: Damn Gene no.

The conversation then continues with the unabridged version of all the guilty parties. He will say he is mad, then identify the next person on the list, reiterate, "Me present no," and continue until each and every offending party has been named. The fact that the individual might be out of town, on his/her deathbed, or stranded aboard the international space station IS NO EXCUSE. Note to any perspective member of the birthday club – money is the preferred gift.

It is not an accident that the name Gene was chosen in the previous scenario – nor is it an accident that the word "damn" was used with his name.

Gene Owens is a Clinton High graduate. He was a well-respected science teacher at Clinton Middle School and a well-respected assistant principal at Clinton High School. He is a member of the East Tennessee Baseball Coaches Hall of Fame. For years he coached baseball with another Hall of Fame coach – Alvin Taylor. And he is a great example of the power of Freddy's speech.

For years, Freddy chased foul balls for the baseball team. For years, Coach Taylor paid him to do so. Then, in 1986, Alvin went to Anderson County to coach basketball.

The move led to Gene Owens becoming the head coach at C.H.S. His assistant coach was Jim Payne. Both men knew their baseball, and both men knew Freddy, but neither man had any idea that Alvin had been giving Freddy five dollars per game; in fact neither gave it a thought until the end of the first game. That's when it occurred to Coach Owens that Freddy needed to be compensated. He consulted with his trusted assistant and concluded that he probably got one dollar.

Freddy was not pleased with his reduction in pay. The phrase, "One damn dollar" would be repeated frequently. In fact, Coach Taylor would receive a phone call from his favorite ball chaser. "I mad" was the typical opening salvo, followed by, "I mad damn Gene." Damn Gene and one damn dollar quickly became a major theme of the conversation. And Jim Payne was not to escape damnation either, except Freddy had a different expletive for him. His intent was to lay the "f-word" on Coach Payne, only it came out, "Buck Payne."

Jim Payne was a talented football and track athlete at Central High School. He taught special education in Anderson County for many years until he retired. His unique sense of humor has made him a popular figure in Knoxville and Clinton. He was known as Jimbo to those who knew him in high school, but once Freddy dubbed him Buck Payne, the nickname stuck. So did the moniker Damn Gene.

Long after peace had been made, long after the important financial negotiations had been resolved, the nicknames stuck, once again demonstrating the unique power of one unique individual.

In many situations, the cussing might be considered offensive. Somehow, when Freddy does it, it becomes acceptable. To their credit, both coaches have accepted the nicknames with typical good-natured humor.

It is now quite common for friends to ask about Damn Gene's health or whereabouts. The same is true for Buck Payne. It is extraordinary that one incident in Freddy World can have such a permanent impact.

There is a footnote to this story. When Jim and his wife Gwen had a baby girl, they named her Julia. From the time of her birth until the present, this college-aged woman has been known in Freddy World by a term only he could create. The term? Baby Buck. What else would it be?

Angela

"I am not a very emotional person. . ." she pauses, her expressive brown eyes darting as she searches for just the right words. She begins again. "I am not an emotional person until it comes to Freddy." Her eyes are no longer darting as they take on a softer, moister quality.

One precious childhood moment occurred when she was three. The moment happened when her two older brothers decided to hone their skills as barbers. Angela had never had a haircut. She had long hair. Middle of the back length hair. Beautiful hair.

When it was over, she still had long hair – on the sides. Some still hung to her shoulders. But in the back – in the very middle of the back, a huge chunk was missing. In today's terms, it was the equivalent of a reverse mullet. Angela preened down the stairs, getting her mother's attention with the word, "Look." Barbara looked. Barbara saw. Barbara spanked her budding barbers.

Even though she is four years younger, Angela Poole personifies the protective big sister. It is a deeply-rooted instinct that may have its origin in an early childhood experience. She recalls being a student at Clinton Elementary School and seeing a young boy being picked on. He was called a retard. She remembers how hurtful that word was, and still is. She remembers feeling that he just needed a friend. She would proudly be that friend. It would not be her last experience with cruelty.

Freddy calls her Wahl-Way, and her earliest memories are of

the family playing in the snow, using socks for mittens. She recalls how remarkable it was that his balance seemed so good back then. They were good times, innocent times, the halcyon days of laughter and ching-chong (Freddy's word for ice cream). It was a *Leave it to Beaver* world, and it would not last.

Angela would learn that her little friend at Clinton Elementary School was not the only one who would experience the prejudice that comes from fear and ignorance. She would learn that some of her friends were not allowed to play at her house because Freddy was there. Even her husband, Steven Poole, was not immune from the misinformation campaign. Angela recalls his incredulous reaction when he learned that she was Freddy's sister. Steven had been told that Freddy was dangerous. Of course, he would eventually learn the truth – that Freddy is not the least bit dangerous. It is misinformation that is dangerous. It can create beliefs based on groundless assumptions. It can be harmful and hurtful.

Steven – whose name is pronounced Chee-ken by his brother-in-law – now knows the truth. Moving past the negativity, the stereotypes, and the misconceptions can lead to the happiness and humor a person like Freddy can create. Chee-ken now knows and loves a person who was once considered a taboo – a person to be avoided. But how many people never have that opportunity? How many continue to live lives rooted in false assumptions about those who are different? Isn't that the way that all prejudicial treatment begins?

Like *The Clinton 12*, Freddy was never allowed to attend Clinton public schools. He was sent to the now closed Daniel Arthur Rehabilitation Center in Oak Ridge, and while that facility enjoyed a positive reputation, it was a shocking experience for Freddy. He was placed with the more profound cases – children who drooled, who wore diapers, who did not have the energy or the social skills he possessed. And, as Angela points out, Freddy had never been treated differently. "He was just one of us." He would eventually rebel.

Angela teaches at Norwood Middle School. As an educator, she can't help but wonder what might have been had her oldest brother grown up in a different time. Today, his educational program and opportunities would be greater. Still, it could have been worse. At least the family did not follow the advice of the educator who recommended Freddy be institutionalized, that the pleasant-sounding Green Valley in Greenville, Tennessee would be the best place for him, that the family, especially the girls, would be safer that way.

Angela and her family have survived the archaic thinking of a time gone by. She knows it would be a mistake to view the beauty of Freddy's relationship with Clinton as it exists today and assume that it has always been that way. It has not.

"He has a lot of fears," she murmurs, her eyes darting again. "He is afraid of falling. He is afraid of being hurt." Those fears are well-founded. There would be dark days, even violent days. But there would also be a caring sister to offer love, and support, and ching-chong.

Here, There, and Everywhere

U – biq – ui – tous (adjective)
Present, appearing, or found everywhere. (Merriam Webster On-
line Dictionary)

If ever a word was perfect for a person, ubiquitous is the match for
Freddy, especially the younger version. He was everywhere. His
rounds included the Little China Restaurant, Hoskins Drug Store,
Hammers Department Store, the Apple Blossom Café (and Miller's
Restaurant before that), the Ritz Theatre, Mitchell's Hair Salon,
Los Caballeros Mexican Restaurant, and any other establishment
willing to welcome him.

It might get loud, it might get silly, but it would always be
interesting. Occasionally, it would be touching.

Carolin Lefevers knows about touching experiences. The veteran
Clinton High School worker reports, "I have a grandson with Down
syndrome. He does not have the usual appearance that most of
these special children have. Especially as a toddler, unless you were
aware of his diagnosis, no one really knew. My husband and I took
Zach to Miller's Restaurant for dinner." Miller's was the forerunner
to today's Apple Blossom Café. "We were sitting at our table and
Freddy came over. He was enamored with Zachary, and I just
watched him play with him. After a little while, Freddy looked up
smiling grandly, as if to say, 'He's special.' I just wanted to cry, but
all I could do was smile, because Freddy's special, too.'"

The story demonstrates two remarkable truths. First, Freddy is welcome at virtually any table, with any family, anywhere. And secondly, it shows he is far smarter and more sensitive than some might suspect.

Dean Brock knows about ubiquitous Freddy. The Brock family is responsible for the restoration of a Clinton landmark – The Ritz Theatre. Like so many other places in town, Freddy is always welcome there. A free movie and free popcorn are hard to turn down. Dean recalls seeing movies with Freddy in the audience. Sometimes, something in a movie might strike his celebrity guest as funny. Uninhibited, unbridled laughter would follow, and if no one else was laughing – well . . . so what?

Dean's favorite story is a classic. "I was taking tickets at the door one day when Freddy walked by. I opened the door and invited him in. Just as he was walking through the door, I heard a LOUD pop. Like a .45 caliber pop. It scared me so bad I about jumped out of my skin. I saw Freddy squint and he fell backwards holding his stomach. I thought, 'Holy shit! Someone's shot Freddy!' I'm leaning over him, asking him where it hurts, worried out of my mind, when Freddy, still lying on his back, points his finger at me and laughs that laugh of his. As I helped him up, I realized the pop must have been a backfire from a passing truck, which obviously scared both of us. Freddy just happened to realize everything was ok before I did. Yup, I got punked by Freddy."

In Freddy World, lots of people seem to spend lots of time just shattin' 'round. Of course, Freddy himself can be a world class shatter. He does much of his shattin' at The Apple Blossom Cafe, usually at HIS table. It is in the far left corner as you enter. He sits there, sometimes alone, sometimes with company. Other times he begins his sojourn at his table, but joins others who arrive. He is not opposed to yelling someone's name. A common greeting from Freddy is, "Oh no." Even if he is happy to see you, "Oh no" is often said. Or, "Oh gee." Or, "Go home." Or, "You out." Or, "Oh my God." It just depends. Sometimes the "Oh" has 32 syllables.

And then, it would be off to some event somewhere with some

kind Clintonian. It might be a sporting event, or the fair, a trip to the community center, or Hooters. That's right, Hooters. Whatever the case, the odds are that ubiquitous Freddy is not just shattin' 'round for long – not if there are places to go and people to see.

People have been known to say good-bye to Freddy at one event, get in their car to drive to another event, only to find Freddy already there. The reason that happens is simple. There are many people who delight in his company, who will transport him to any place he needs to go. The world is his chauffer, at least the world in Clinton, Tennessee.

Wrestling with Rhodey

Jason Rhodey graduated from Clinton High School in 1993. He played on some of Clinton's best football teams, and he worked at Freddy's favorite store, Hammers. Those two facts are enough to qualify Jason for star status in Freddy World, and earn him the moniker "Football Boy." His father, Steve, would be known as, "Football Boy's Daddy." Jason is not only the Football Boy, but he is clearly the favorite – and for good reason.

Freddy's loves are simple. He loves his family and friends. He loves Christmas and his birthday. He loves Clinton sports and the Anderson County Fair. But his love for wrestling reaches fanatical proportions. Jason Rhodey became a professional wrestler, and, in the process, elevated his already considerable status.

Jason has known Freddy for about twenty-five years. His earliest memories involve Freddy watching him in T-ball. He admits to being afraid of Freddy at first, but quickly learned there was nothing to fear. By the time he was a high school student, he realized how much fun it was to have Freddy around.

From 1999 -- 2002, Jason wrestled under the name of Jason Justice. Sometimes he would have a tag-team partner, Scott Bishop. When that happened, they called themselves the U.S. Marshalls. Of course, the U.S. Marshalls needed a flag, and it is impossible to have a flag without someone to carry and wave it, so . . . drum roll . . . Enter Freddy. There were wrestling matches in Clinton, Knoxville, Lenoir City, and Rockwood. There were even matches in Kentucky.

And at every stop, Freddy became a star. As Jason observes, "There were times when Freddy WAS the show; that he was more entertaining than the wrestlers."

All the wrestlers loved Freddy. They would yell and tease him because they knew he would yell back. A favorite ploy was to get him riled up enough to stand on a chair, take off his shirt, whip it over his head, and then throw it in the ring. The crowd would reach frenzied heights. And then the shirtless manager of the U.S. Marshalls would flex. He would pose. He would strike the fiercest body builder pose he could muster. And the crowd would go wild. Jason has the D.V.D. to prove it – and it is "must see T.V."

Jason recalls a time when the shirt almost didn't come off. That was because it got stuck on a certain belt – a replica of the old W.C.W. (World Champion Wrestling) belt with a huge buckle. Jason was there when Freddy paid $150.00 for the belt. He was there when it was discovered that Freddy was carrying an amazing total of $1,600.00 at the time. Fortunately, the days of him carrying that kind of money are long gone.

One of Freddy's favorite professional wrestlers was Bullet Bob Armstrong. Freddy had the entire costume – boots, suit, and mask. It doubled as a Halloween costume. Current Clinton High School baseball coach, Casey Taylor, remembers the costumed crusader getting very angry when someone pulled off his mask. Clearly, some things are just not okay. As Jim Croce might have sung, "You don't tug on Superman's cape, you don't spit into the wind, you don't pull the mask off of Bullet Bob Fagan, and you don't mess around with Jim."

You also don't chest bump Freddy when he comes strolling down the ramp at Hammers original site on Market Street. Jason learned that the hard way – although it wasn't hard for Jason. He recalls that Freddy's all-time favorite wrestler was Nature Boy Ric Flair. It seems that the Nature Boy had a certain strut and scream – a war hoop – that Freddy loved to imitate. He also liked to slap ten – (anyone can slap a measly five) and chest bump. When the Football Boy played along with the chest bump, Freddy was sent flying into the outside storage area. He wasn't seriously hurt, but it warranted a stern reprimand from Jason's boss. Which is only fair. If anyone has Freddy's back, it is Hammers' manager Don Calhoun.

Hammer Time

The official name is Hammer's Stores, LLC. There are ten of them. The first one opened in Guntersville, Alabama in 1942. A decade later, Clinton, Tennessee would have one.

Hammers is a discount store, a gathering place, a local treasure, and a mecca for people in surrounding communities. People will travel many miles to participate in one of Hammers numerous sales. These sales are an event. It is common for people to be lined up outside – waiting for the store to open. Few businesses are as closely connected to a community as Hammers is to Clinton. Few businessmen are as closely connected to their town in the manner that Hammers leadership is. And few people know and care for and love Freddy like Don Calhoun does.

Don Calhoun is the manager of this piece of Americana. His knowledge of and love for movies and sports and Clinton history make him a fascinating conversationalist. But it is his knowledge of and love for Freddy that make him one of the most important people in Freddy's life.

Don's name has been changed in Freddy's world. He is John. John is married to the former Margaret Hammer. If Margaret's name is attempted at all, it usually comes out as, "Gargret." More often, she is referred to as, "John's Girl." Don and Margaret have a son named Kelley – pronounced, "Cruddy." Cruddy's wife, Tonya, is Cruddy's girl. Their children are Cruddy's boys.

Margaret's mother, Helen, still works at the store and still can be seen in commercials for it. To most, she is Mrs. Hammer. To Freddy, she is known as, "Chief." She is so strongly associated with the store that bears her name, and that of her late husband Bernard, that she has received correspondences addressed to Mrs. Hammers.

The Chief has a desk in her office. There is only one person in Clinton who would dare to walk into her office, sit in her chair, and put his feet on her desk. Of course, she isn't there when he does, but it demonstrates the comfort level he has there.

Don's first recollection of Freddy involves an incident at a grocery store that no longer exists – The White Store. While Don was shopping in the store, a ten-year-old Freddy came in, grabbed a bag of chips, and walked out. The owner called the police. There is no record of Freddy doing any time for this offense, but it may have been part of the ten-year-old's "crime spree." Angela Poole, one of his two sisters, recalls how her brother went into their father's wallet, took one hundred dollars, and went shopping. Neighborhood children received a treasure-trove of "free" toys. He did get in trouble for that incident, but not with the police.

Freddy's potential life of crime may have been halted years later, and Don Calhoun may have stopped it. Hammers had received a supply of athletic shirts -- shirts that needed to be sorted. Freddy had started hanging around the store, and he would occasionally help. On the day he helped sort the athletic clothing, he became enamored with a referee's shirt. Don decided that he would give him the shirt as payment for his work, but he never got the chance. When Freddy left, he helped himself to the shirt.

It is possible that one of the closest relationships in Clinton began when Don called Freddy and insisted that he return the shirt, which he did. A stern lecture followed as Don explained that he could not have that kind of behavior in his store. The shirt was held until the proper time – a time when it had been earned. Then it was given as a gift. That was more than three decades ago. Don has never had another problem with that type of behavior.

Of course there is a story behind why Freddy began to hang out at Hammers in the first place. Sometime around 1976, after a long, bitter cold spell, a woman rushed into the store to seek help for a young man bleeding in the streets. It was Freddy, who had fallen and cut his head. Don called an ambulance and Freddy's mother. He went to see him at the hospital, and after that, a casual acquaintance became an increasingly close friendship. It would be several more years before the referee's shirt helped to strengthen that friendship.

The referee's shirt would be worn around town for many years, and it was likely the shirt of choice when Freddy halted a Clinton Middle School basketball game – twice. Retired biology teacher John Byrd was coaching that day. The game was underway, and suddenly a whistle blew. John recalls, "Everybody stopped. Nobody moved. The referees just looked at each other – neither of them had blown the whistle." After an awkward pause, the game began again. That's when the coach noticed a certain town favorite chuckling behind the hand covering his mouth. When the whistle stopped play a second time, it became obvious what was happening. The game resumed, and there were no more interruptions, as Freddy watched the rest of the action while sitting next to Coach Byrd on the bench.

The thing about Freddy stories is that they often connect to other stories. Some may seem innocuous enough by themselves, but often they are indicative of significant truths about an individual or a group of people. Don Calhoun allowed Freddy to hang around a place of business when others may have run him off. That speaks volumes about Don. It occurred at a time when Freddy was being teased and treated poorly by some. Donna Parke is the younger of Freddy's two sisters, and she doesn't hesitate to credit Don's taking him in as one of the most significant events in her brother's life. She says, "When Don let him 'work' and hangout there, it made him more accepted. It was very important."

On the surface, it was a single, simple gesture, but the ripples from that gesture would be life changing. "John" had no way of knowing how far his influence would carry. He just knew that he enjoyed Freddy's company. Few people can tell a "Freddy story" better than he can, and few stories have resonated like the one that begins with a simple glass of iced tea.

Tea Good

It was a hot summer day in July. The year was 1988, or maybe 1989, Don isn't one hundred percent sure which. He is sure that it was a Saturday because Saturday was the day he took the checks to the Hammers in Maynardville. And Freddy was along for the ride.

The trip began at the now defunct Little Senator Restaurant/ Drive-In, where the two travelers stopped to eat. It seems that The Little Senator served pitchers of that special Southern nectar – sweet iced tea. Cold iced tea – delicious iced tea. During the lunch, Don wasn't really paying attention to how much tea his companion was consuming , at least not initially. He does recall that their glasses were frequently being refilled, and that after every refill Freddy would exclaim, "Tea good." Eventually, it registered that, "Tea good" was an oft repeated refrain – and that maybe that wasn't a good thing.

After the meal, they got into Don's Toyota – the one with the nice leather seats. They made it to Maynardville without incident. Freddy used the bathroom before they headed back, but the return trip would create an instant classic.

The journey between Clinton and Maynardville consists of long stretches of road that are bumpy, winding, and narrow. Some sections have no shoulder – no possible place to stop or pull over. In fact, on some of the steepest s-curves, pulling over might mean leaving the road and plunging off a cliff. It was on just such a stretch that Freddy yelled, "John – me gotta go!" There was nothing "John" could do, even with the repeated mantra, "Me gotta go" echoing in his ears. By the time he was able to get to a safe spot, Freddy no longer had to go.

All Don could think to say was, "Fred – tea good?" Freddy's response? "Shut up, John."

Nobody has tried to embarrass Freddy about this incident, but the story has been told and retold so often that many adults in Clinton will think and/or verbalize "tea good" every time they have iced tea. That's the thing about Freddy stories. They not only last, they actually change the way people think and speak and react. This story is more than twenty years old, yet saying those two magic words will cause people to smile, or laugh, or repeat another classic Freddy story. Who else has that kind of impact?

Donna

For many years, she was the baby of the family, at least until John was born. In Freddyspeak, baby is pronounced B.B., and this B.B. shines. Her vivacious, friendly manner and warm personality are magnified the moment her oldest brother's name is mentioned.

Donna remembers Freddy learning to tie his shoes – no small task with one useable hand. And she remembers the bike. Freddy loved to ride his bike, and he would do so for hours. Again, no small task for someone with one functional arm. She remembers him often being banged up from his accidents.

She remembers trying to teach him to read. She was eight, and Freddy was fourteen, and it was one of the rare times when she and her brother shared the feeling of frustration. He learned to recognize the word "wagon." That was the extent of her tutorial success.

Like all of her siblings, she remembers him sneaking out of the house. He would tiptoe to the back door and leave. He hated feeling confined. That is why, from an early age, he was seen all over town – walking as a youngster, riding his bike when he got older.

She remembers a time when Freddy accidently poured boiling water on his chest, and hid the fact because he thought he might get into trouble.

She remembers going to a Waffle House in Nashville, near Opryland, and people recognizing Freddy there.

She remembers the pain of her father leaving, and the scars her family shared. She recalls the lip quiver that indicates Freddy is really upset – and that his lip quivered often during that time.

It is interesting to note that Freddy often says he is mad at someone, but he usually isn't really mad. In fact, it is his closest friends who make him mad, and that is often quickly rectified. The reality is that he can sound almost happy when he tells you about his "madness." But when he is really upset, hurt or picked on – or when his father left – his face changes. He frowns, and his upper lip starts to quiver.

She remembers the daily battles that occurred when Freddy resisted going to Daniel Arthur, the facility that would provide most of Freddy's training. There were days when it was a minor skirmish. There were days when it was major combat.

Donna, like all of her siblings, also recalls the incredulous look and tone people would have when they asked, "Freddy's your brother?" She recalls the people who have teased him – some good-naturedly, some not. One of the teasers was Chuck Parke – the man she would marry. Spend any time with Chuck and it becomes abundantly clear – Chuck loves his brother-in-law. In the spirit of full disclosure, he confessed to an isolated incident where he joined others who used Curtis Mayfield's song *Freddy's Dead* to tease him. It was the type of thing that being young and foolish may foster. Sometime later, he would see others do a similar thing, and it angered him. He would go from one-time teaser to full-time protector. Such is the transformative power of Freddy Fagan.

Donna remembers a time, in the early 80's, when she was in college and her mom had surgery at Vanderbilt Hospital. Freddy was forced to stay with his Uncle Carl in Nashville. He was miserable – he just sat around, listless, a lifeless young man. It was at that moment that she realized how uniquely beautiful Clinton is. She points out, "Freddy couldn't survive in Nashville – or many other places, either."

And that's something Donna often thinks about. She knows how lucky the Fagan family is to have lived in Clinton. She is grateful to the many people who have been in it for "the long term" – who did, and continue to do things for Freddy not because it is a chore, but because it is something they enjoy. She believes she has seen Freddy soften others.

She is especially grateful to two men who came into Freddy's life when he was being picked on and changed the public perception. She credits Don Calhoun for allowing Freddy to "work" at Hammers when so many others might have run him off. "It allowed him to feel like he had a job. It allowed people to see the other side of Freddy."

She pauses, then speaks about the man who, with one small gesture, may have permanently changed the perception of her oldest brother. It happened in Jaycee Park, at the swimming pool. Freddy became an honorary lifeguard, and the ripples from that moment are still being felt. "It was Alvin Taylor who put a whistle around his neck. That was THE CHANGE."

Taylor Made

"You can tell everything you need to know about a person by the way he or she reacts to Freddy." With that one simple aphorism, Alvin Taylor crystallizes a truth for many Clintonians. He should know. It is impossible to overstate the impact he has had on Freddy – or the impact Freddy has had on him.

Alvin is a Clinton High graduate – in fact, he was voted Mr. C.H.S. his senior year. He has had a Hall of Fame career as a baseball coach. He has also coached basketball. He was a well-respected English teacher before becoming an administrator. He is on the C.H.S. Wall of Fame.

In 1975, he and his wife, Diane, moved into a house across the street from the Fagans. In typical Fredcabulary style, Diane became Bye Ran. Alvin was, is, and will always be "Coach." When Coach and Bye Ran had a son, they named him Casey. Freddy renamed him Cray Cray. Cray Cray grew up and married a woman who everyone not named Freddy refers to as Kelly. To Freddy, she is Cruddy. When they got a dog, they named it Rookie. Crookie is Freddy's interpretation. A typical Fredism might include Coach and Bye Ran taking Crookie for a walk while Cray Cray and Cruddy went on vacation. Any questions?

Alvin got to witness Freddy at home. He became the manager of the Jaycee Pool – and he got to see him there. When he became the Dragon's head baseball coach, they got to spend even more quality time together. Over time, one of the most enduring and unique relationships would develop – accompanied by some classic stories.

Not long after the Taylors moved in, some time in the mid 70's, Alvin was awakened in the middle of the night by a loud noise coming from the Fagan's house. Curious, he got dressed and went outside. The noise was coming from a lawnmower that Freddy had started. Alvin approached the "handyman" and asked what he was doing. He was informed that Freddy was going to mow the lawn. Alvin responded, "Freddy, it's the middle of the night. Why don't you wait until the daytime?"

Freddy's response? "Too damn hot!"

How does one argue with logic like that? Of course the idea of Freddy using a lawnmower is . . . well . . . interesting. And yet, it does show a determination to be just like everyone else.

Alvin got to witness the Daniel Arthur van, honking and waiting while Freddy hid or just plain refused to go. But it was at the Jaycee Pool where their special bond really began.

It was summer, and it was hot. There were times when Freddy would show up at the pool with less than stellar grooming. "Gamy" is Alvin's word for it. He would insist that Freddy shower. He would shave him. Eventually, he would make him an honorary lifeguard – shirt and swim trunks included. And the whistle – especially the whistle. Over time, through the efforts of the lifeguards, Freddy was accepted. He relished the attention. He was "working." He was important. It was as if those who frequented the pool saw him differently. Freddy became cool – and treating him well became fashionable. It has remained that way for well over three decades now. Like Donna Parke said, "Putting a whistle around his neck was THE CHANGE."

Lifeguarding was not the only job Alvin would give Freddy. He would pay him to retrieve foul balls during Clinton High baseball games, a job Freddy did with pride. When he was younger, he moved with amazing speed, and he saved the Dragons a good deal of money by finding baseballs that might otherwise have been lost.

When the baseball team had an away game, Freddy rode the bus. Other coaches in other sports would follow that example, too. It was the beginning of Freddy becoming a fixture at every C.H.S. sporting event. It was the beginning of other coaches in other schools learning to appreciate him as well.

How significant is Alvin's making him part of the baseball program, and other coaches joining in? By the time Jim Davis become the athletic director in the 2000's, he states, "At every away game, the very first question I was asked by the other athletic director was either, 'Where's Freddy?' or 'Is Freddy coming?'"

Alvin and Freddy talk on the phone daily. Sometimes there are numerous phone calls each day. No one "translates" those difficult to understand words and phrases better than Alvin.

He has seen Freddy in the baseball team's batting cage, holding a bat and saying, "Me Chipper Jones." He's heard classic messages on his answering machine, like Freddy's Valentine message reminding Alvin to get Diane some flowers to show her his love. The message? "Bye Ran rose? Rove you."

After the confusion over Damn Gene and the one dollar payment, Freddy told Alvin, "Me coach – Gene foul balls." It seemed like a fair role reversal.

Occasionally, Alvin has had to go to bat for Freddy at baseball games. Most veteran umpires know Freddy and get a good laugh at his antics, but not always. Once, at an Oak Ridge game, as Freddy was yelling, "Strike" before every pitch, an unappreciative umpire stopped the game, and announced, "Whoever is calling balls and strikes, stop it now." This was met with a great deal of laughter from the fans, and even from the other umpire. Freddy was beyond mad – he was pissed, or perhaps "pished." This was a red-faced lip-twitching anger. For two years, Freddy refused to go to the Oak Ridge game. In his mind, that same umpire would be there.

A week or two later, there was a junior varsity game in Clinton. Guess who was the umpire? Freddy was yelling and carrying on. The ump called the junior varsity coach – Football Boy Jason Rhodey – out onto the field. (This was during Rhodey's pre-wrestling period.) He informed Jason that Freddy was about to be thrown out. Jason found Alvin and informed him of what was going on. The "conversation" that followed between the umpire and Alvin was very one-sided.

"You are not throwing him out of the park," was the introduction, the supporting evidence, and the conclusion. It was repeated a few times for emphasis. The umpire's protestations and explanations were interrupted with, "I'm telling you, you are not kicking Freddy out. He's been doing this for thirty years. You will not kick him out." This is the P.G. version of the discussion, but when it was over, justice prevailed. Freddy remained.

At the conclusion of the game, Freddy, who had adjourned to the press box, happened to come down just as the umpire walked behind the press box. Those close enough heard Freddy say two words that have earned their way into folk legend status. The words? "Damn jackass."

Ray Blakeney recently retired as the sports editor for the local newspaper, *The Clinton Courier News*. He says that umpires now receive "Freddy Training" at their annual meeting. They are told to expect a loud, harmless fan. They are taught to ignore it. In fact, the head of the umpire's association usually finds Freddy and gives him a present at the first ball game. The present? A t-shirt, what else?

Alvin had Freddy's back – at the ball field, at the pool, and anywhere else he was needed. It is true, you can tell all you need to know about a person by the way he or she reacts to Freddy. The way that Alvin Taylor reacts makes him a superstar.

Off the Deep End

Jaycee Pool isn't just a place where Freddy became accepted. It is a place for many adventures, or misadventures, and a few close calls. Steve Pyatt can attest to that.

As the owner of the insurance company that bears his name, as a former member of the Anderson County Fair Association, and as basketball referee, Mr. Pyatt has had many dealings with Freddy. He is being quite literal when he says, "I've known Freddy my entire life." They are the same age. He can't pinpoint his earliest memory, but he's certain it had something to do with a bike, or a ball field, or both. He recalls numerous bike wrecks, and how Freddy always seemed to jump up, unfazed, ready to ride again. But his most vivid memory occurred at the bottom of the Jaycee Pool.

It was around 1974 or '75, and Steve was working as a lifeguard. He was on duty, even though no one was actually in the water at the time. He remembers seeing Freddy walking around the pool. He remembers looking away – scanning the area the way a vigilant guard should. He recalls that, when he looked back, toward the deep end, Freddy was not in sight. Then he looked down into the water – and he knew where Freddy was.

Freddy can not swim. Mr. Pyatt did what lifeguards are trained to do – he dove in. What happened next was both horrifying and humorous at the same time. Pyatt reached the bottom and found Freddy actually STANDING there – in ten feet of water – arms folded, as if he didn't have a care in the world. He was simply looking around, or, as Steve describes it, "It was like he was standing on the corner, waiting for a bus. There was no buoyancy at all."

The word lifeguard takes on new meaning in a case like this. Someone was literally guarding Freddy's life – and promptly brought him to the surface. Somehow, he inhaled no water – was not really that scared or upset. He never really panicked while he was under water.

Over time, as the nervousness of what might have been receded, the visual of Freddy standing on the bottom of the Jaycee Pool has created one of those stories that is told and retold – and will continue to be retold for generations.

Eventually, Freddy would wear one of the matching lifeguard uniforms. He would have the whistle – he would even yell at people for running or splashing. And he found another reason to frequent the pool.

In those days, the pool closed at 6:00 p.m. The concession stand would, invariably, have unsold hot dogs leftover. Somehow, the boy who cannot tell time found a way to arrive just before closing – when the hot dogs were being passed out. Of course, some days he never left, so that made it easy. It is another example of his uncanny abilities.

Steve has dealt with Freddy in many capacities, but few are more telling than the frequent visits he would receive at his office. Before the hip injury slowed him down, Pyatt's Insurance was a frequent stop. He would come in to visit with the office staff, to drink a free soft drink, and to watch the T.V. in the waiting room. It was just one more place where he was always welcome, one more stop on his appointed rounds, and one more place where he could feel safe. After all, there was a lifeguard on duty.

Miller Time

Freddy spends a great deal of time at the Apple Blossom Café. His attendance there is part habit, part tradition, and some sort of cosmic, divine ritual. It is a ceremonial rite with a long history.

The Apple Blossom's roots began in 1972, when a retired postal worker named Chuck Miller and his wife, Katherine, opened Miller's restaurant on Market Street. From the onset it was, and continues to be, a family restaurant – a gathering place with a friendly, informal atmosphere and good, "down home" cooking. It wasn't until 1977 that a new building was built – a building that would become a fixture in Clinton. The new location was not far from the original site – and both sites were within walking distance for Freddy.

The Millers would run the restaurant until 1984. They came back in 1994 and ran it again until 2000.

The Millers have four sons – Rick, Randy, Roger, and Ronnie, but numerous people have suggested that Freddy was their oldest son. That's because they treated him like family – and because he was often there. And, when Katherine speaks about Freddy, there is a decided maternal quality to her comments.

Freddy calls Katherine, "The Judge." She isn't sure why, but she speculates that it might have something to do with a few times she had to be stern, especially where his hygiene was concerned.

There are times, especially in the summer, when, if he gets careless or forgetful, Freddy can have some issues with his grooming, especially as it relates to body odor. Numerous people have helped him address this problem. They have seen to it that he bathed, that he washed his hair. Some have actually shaved him. Don Calhoun is one of those people. Alvin Taylor is another. Katherine Miller has, on occasion, told Freddy that he needed to clean up before entering her restaurant. She has taken him home so he could do so. She has picked him up after he has done so. Sometimes he is perfectly fine with being directed in this manner – sometimes he is not pleased. But even if he is not happy, that will eventually change – especially if free food is to follow.

It is difficult to calculate how many free meals Miller's provided – or how many the Apple Blossom continues to provide. It is not uncommon for him to eat his three daily meals there.

Chuck Miller passed away in 2005. Katherine fondly recalls how her late husband loved to tease Freddy, how he loved to be with him. She quickly and proudly points out that a certain part of Chuck survives today. Like the most protective of mothers, she was, and continues to be concerned with the basics – food, clothing and shelter. And to that end, Chuck made sure that Freddy would be well dressed if he needed to go to a church service or a wedding or a funeral. Often, he will be seen in a light green suit – Chuck's light green suit.

Katherine has known Freddy for forty years. She has taken him to church. She has played the piano while Freddy sang *Amazing Grace*. She has fed him breakfast in the morning and taken him home after closing. She has also put him to work. He has occasionally picked up dishes for her, but his main job was that of messenger.

In a time before cell phones, a working mom with four active boys might have difficulty communicating with her children. Enter the Fagan Express. Katherine laughs as she recalls, "Freddy would take notes to my boys. If one was at the community center or at a ball field, I'd write him a note, tell Freddy where to take it, and off he'd go." When Freddy found the designated son, he would yell, "Hey Boy – Judge want you." Then he'd deliver the message and the "boy" would go home, or do whatever the note instructed.

Katherine's restaurant days are over now. She spends much of her time in Florida. But those golden days are never far from her mind. And she is willing to confirm an often rumored detail about the sale of Miller's Restaurant. When she and Chuck sold their place to Brenda and Von Hudson, they did, indeed, have a stipulation in the contract that Freddy would continue to eat – free of charge – at the new owner's establishment. The Hudsons would change the name to The Apple Blossom Café, but Freddy would still be welcome. To Katherine, it was very basic; "I just wanted to make sure he was fed."

In a small, Southern town, a teenage boy enters a family restaurant. He leaves indelible marks on the hearts of the family members – so much so that they help clean him and clothe him and feed him. He becomes so important to them that his well-being is a contractual stipulation in a financial transaction. This kind of concern and caring is praise-worthy, perhaps even inspiring. But it is hardly unique – not in Clinton, Tennessee.

John

"In my heart, being Freddy's brother is an honor." So says the youngest of the five Fagan siblings – John. He adds, "It's hard to explain if you haven't grown up with it . . . you just feel for anyone who is challenged."

John is fifteen years younger than his oldest brother. He served in the Navy during Desert Storm, and now works at the Norris Post Office. His is one of the few names Freddy pronounces correctly, although sometimes he is called, "My John" to differentiate between others called John. Daughter Gwyneth is either "John's girl" or "My John's girl."

John readily admits that he is more often known as Freddy's brother than by his own name. He says, "If it wasn't for Freddy, not many people would know me." His earliest childhood memory involves the tears he shed after his finger was caught in a BB gun Freddy had difficulty cocking, and the sympathy flowing with the reported word "sorry," as in, "Me sorry, John." The gun was a natural, given Freddy's love of cowboys, although using the words Freddy and BB gun in the same sentence is a little scary.

The gun belonged to Joe, and John had no way of knowing that it had already gotten his two brothers in trouble. Before John was born, when Freddy was about ten, Freddy used Joe's gun for target practice. Unfortunately, the target turned out to be the windows of Evans Construction Company. Joe bore the brunt of that punishment.

John recalls Freddy wearing a cowboy hat and cowboy boots and going to a place in Florida called Six Gun Territory, where hourly reenactments of gun fights thrilled his cowboy partner.

He also recalls a poignantly negative moment, when a sixth grade argument ended with an adversary saying, "Well at least I don't have a retarded brother." It was the only time he had heard such a comment, and it hurt. "I was torn up, crying. . ." He doesn't finish. He doesn't have to. Fortunately, he can quickly turn to more pleasant events – like letting Freddy attempt to drive his truck – an event that ended with John stomping on the brake before they went off an embankment. It was Freddy's first and last driving experience with John.

When Joe Fagan moved to Florida, two significant consequences occurred. The first was the increase in John's responsibility for Freddy's health and well-being, especially since the hip injury. Freddy takes seven pills daily. "Pills good" is Freddy's way of assuring John he has taken his medicine. He does it every morning. Sometimes he calls John at work. If things are busy, he has to put Freddy on hold. He has gotten wrapped up in work enough to actually forget that someone important is waiting for him. He has gone fifteen or twenty minutes, maybe even longer. But when he remembers, Freddy is still patiently waiting. There is something touching about that.

The second consequence of Joe's move was the opportunity to visit Florida and to fish. Joe's house sits so close to an inlet that they can literally fish off the back porch. Freddy loves to fish, and on one particular visit, he caught several catfish. The essence of Freddy's child-like innocence and unbridled enthusiasm was captured in those moments. John describes it this way: "Every fish was like he was catching his first fish ever."

The hip injury took a toll on everyone. Freddy was hurt, and ultimately, depressed. For several months, rumors circulated. "It seems like everyone was asking about him," says John. He adds, "Even now, two years later, Freddy will say, 'Me walking.'" It's as if he is reminding himself that he is finally okay.

Bob Williams and John Fagan share an interesting insight about Freddy's phone call decorum. It is often true that, after saying good-bye, but before hanging up, Freddy will make a final comment – a Shakespearean soliloquy of sorts. He might offer an insight into what he is thinking. For example, if John has asked him to do something he doesn't want to do, he might hear, "Me no." Bob once overheard, "Me damn game, no" when he had invited Freddy to a Lady Vols basketball game. If Freddy is not alone, he may tell anyone close enough to listen something about the caller. Fortunately, it is usually positive.

John admits to worrying about Freddy, but says, "The town puts your mind at ease." That is the ultimate compliment from this compassionate individual. He adds, "I'm so proud of him, and all he's accomplished. Having Freddy in my life has given me a sense of purpose. He is that one constant. He will always be the same."

The Bachelor Pad

Since 1984, Freddy has lived in a place called The Towers – a rather presumptuous title for a long, flat building, although, with a whopping five stories, it does tower over most of the buildings in Clinton. And even though it is one building, it is still called The Towers – plural.

The building is privately owned by Lawler-Wood, but it receives federal funding from HUD because it houses the elderly and people with disabilities. There are 149 apartments in the building. Almost all of them are single occupancy. There is only one person who has lived there longer than Freddy. She moved in a year before he did.

Becky Esterkamp is the current manager. She says, "The other tenants love Freddy. They even cook for him." The idea of Freddy finding free food is not surprising, although it can actually be a problem. He now has dietary restrictions that some may not be aware of.

For eight years, Joyce Robbins was the manager. She describes Freddy as, "A sweet, loving person – someone who was a pleasure to be with." She recalls how Freddy would always come to greet new tenants, and how her late husband, Webb, loved to visit. He loved to entertain – to sing at various parties and social functions.

Joyce would cook Thanksgiving and Christmas dinners, organize Halloween parties and summer cookouts. It is little wonder that she became another one of Freddy's many girlfriends. Her boss, owner Don Peterson, always inquired about Freddy, once calling him, "Mr. Clinton."

Joyce spent a lot of time with Joe Fagan. She calls him, "A saint" because of the way he would help his brother.

Freddy used to live on the fourth floor, but after his hip injury, he moved to the first. His apartment is the perfect set-up for him. It has a small kitchen with all of the usual appliances, a well furnished living room, a bedroom, and a bathroom.

The bachelor pad is usually clean, no thanks to the bachelor who lives there. As youngest brother John laughingly observes, "Freddy doesn't clean." John and his mom and the staff of the Towers have plenty of work to do on his behalf.

A visitor to the apartment will notice the sign on the door – Freddy's Place. Upon entering, one will be in the kitchen, by the refrigerator and the sink and the stove. The first item of interest is a large shelf on the left, just before the living room. It contains many valued possessions, including pictures and baseballs and cars. The University of Tennessee football helmet, signed by Coach Phillip Fulmer sits there. So does an autographed photo from legendary U.T. broadcaster John Ward.

The pride of the living room is his new, flat screen T.V. He got it in the summer of 2010 and he immediately got mad at anyone who did not stop by to personally pay homage to it.

He keeps the replica of the World Champion Wrestling belt in his bedroom. The belt is the subject of numerous, contradictory claims, especially concerning who bought it, how many times it has been lost or stolen, and how he got it back. What matters is that he has it now, and it is a prized possession. It is quite heavy, and he likes to show his sense of humor by pretending the belt is too heavy to lift. When he does lift it, he pretends that the belt jerks his arm forward, saying, "Arm broken." The odds are good that there is a radio playing in his room – set to a country music station, most likely Clinton's own WYSH. If the T.V. is on, it too is often set to a country channel. Sometimes the T.V. and the radio compete with each other. But nothing competes with THE

WALL – the wall of shelves that runs floor to ceiling for the length of one entire wall in the bedroom.

Freddy's love of shirts is legendary. "Me shirt" is a phrase so often repeated that it has become a slogan, a mantra, and in some cases, a crusade. Coaches from local sports teams know that providing Freddy with a shirt is an obligation, a rite of passage, and a civic duty. Establishments like Hammers and Hooters seem to have a moral obligation to contribute to the collection. All of this has helped to create a "wall of shirts."

When Freddy had to move from the fourth floor to the first floor, his family members decided to wash, fold, and count all of his prized possessions. The total was an astounding 1,200 shirts. Some are from the mid-80's. Freddy could wear a different shirt every day for more than three years without repeating a shirt. Not that he would. He has favorites that he will wear repeatedly. But that doesn't mean he won't ask for new ones, nor does it mean he will get rid of an old one. And if someone, his mother for instance, has taken a favorite to wash and hasn't returned it promptly, she will hear about it. When it comes to his shirts, Freddy never forgets.

The Towers is the perfect spot for an independent-minded person like Freddy to live. It is truly Freddy's Place.

The Keys to the Kingdom

In most communities, if a person receives the Key to the City, it is a figurative or honorary thing. That is not exactly the case in Clinton.

High on Freddy's list of important items, right up there with shirts and free food and his every-expanding list of girlfriends, is his affinity for keys. He loves keys, and locks, and being the gatekeeper. It is a fascination with fascinating consequences.

James and Ruth Marcum know about Freddy the Gatekeeper. They learned by being band parents – or in their case, band grandparents.

It was a hot day, and the Dragons were playing a home football game. That meant that the band would be playing at halftime. A group of parents (and one set of grandparents) met at the school to load all the cases of soda that had been delivered to the school. Since the football field is a mile from campus, the sodas were being loaded into a van where they could be driven to the football field, unloaded, and iced down for halftime. There were enough sodas for the visiting band as well.

The Marcums don't know exactly how many cases they had, maybe ten to fifteen. They just know that, when they arrived at the field, the gates were all locked, there was no one in sight, and cases of soda were sitting in an increasingly hot van.

James walked across the street to the community center to see if anyone there had a key. No one did, but as he was leaving, one worker offered, "Don't worry. Freddy will be along soon – he'll let you in."

James admits he was skeptical, but he returned to the group of parents and relayed the message. The high school football field is like a "mini-stadium." Surely Freddy would not have a key to such a facility.

Sure enough, as if on cue, Freddy came walking down the street. The conversation went something like this:

James: Freddy, you don't happen to have a key to the stadium, do you?
Freddy: Shoooot yeah.

With that, Freddy reached into his pocket and pulled out the largest ring of keys James had ever seen. Then he did another amazing thing. "He knew exactly which key it was. He just walked over to the lock, and just like that, the gate was open." He still laughs when he thinks about it.

Ruth and her husband love to eat at The Apple Blossom Café, and they especially love to eat with the gatekeeper. He gets a big kick out of being in charge, just like he did when he teased Lisa Harrison Smith about not having the key to the handcuff he placed on her.

Once, during the late 90's, the baseball team was participating in fall ball. The concession stand had been locked up and covered with plywood. When the concession workers went to open it, none of their keys worked. They called for Alvin Taylor – certainly the baseball coach would be able to open it. But he couldn't. That's when Freddy overheard Alvin saying he couldn't open it. That's when he offered, "Me rock it."

By this time, Alvin shouldn't have been surprised by anything Freddy said or did, but he was as he asked, "Freddy, can you open this?"

"Me key" was the response. Detective Taylor would ascertain that Freddy somehow had a key to the old locks. He had gone to Hammers and bought new locks and thrown away the old ones. He was the only person in the town with a key to the baseball concession stand – at least for a short period of time.

He also had a key to the press box. Freddy's time-telling skills are non-existent. He gets so excited about, "Ball game, ball game" that he is always early. He has been seen opening the press box at 1:30 for a 7:30 game.

To some, it may seem odd that Freddy would have so many keys. To others, it is more or less business as usual. But to one woman in Knoxville, the fact that Freddy the Gatekeeper exists is nothing short of a holiday miracle. The following article, reprinted with permission from *The Clinton Courier News*, tells the story.

Giving Back the 'Spirit of Christmas'
By Dan McWilliams

Freddy Fagan may not look like Santa Claus or one of the Christmas Spirits from Charles Dickens' "A Christmas Carol."

He is usually seen wherever Clinton High School athletic teams are – on the sideline cheering on the football Dragons, rooting in the bottom of the seventh or making his impromptu halftime half-court shots.

Or, he can be spotted making the rounds on Market Street, checking locks on doors, making sure Clinton is tucked away safely for the night.

So call him a community-minded citizen, if not a Christmas elf.

But Janet Brooks of Halls knows Fagan and his actions, one in particular, represent the "Spirit of Christmas."

Last Saturday Fagan was checking the locks of Hammer's Store on Market Street when he found an envelope with $270 (five 50s and a 20).

Now, there are a lot of things a lot of different people would have done with that money, but those who know Fagan aren't surprised by his actions.

"He called me at home and told me what he found," Hammer's Manager Don Calhoun said. "He always checks the locks on the door at night and the doors on the van. If there's anything wrong, he calls me at home.

"I've gotten calls from him at 3 a.m. before," Calhoun laughed.

After Fagan called Calhoun and told him about the money the detective work began. See, Fagan was determined to find the rightful owner of the money.

"He kept saying, 'Chris-Chris,'" Calhoun said. "He knew this was someone's Christmas money."

Fagan wouldn't let the envelope with the money tucked safely away inside, out of his sight.

The cash was in a Home Federal envelope and there was a receipt with a code on it, but since there's not a Home Federal in Clinton Fagan and Calhoun journeyed to SunTrust bank and enlisted the help of Phyllis Hill.

Hill contacted Home Federal and, using the number on the receipt, tracked down Brooks.

"She was so happy she was crying," Calhoun said.

So happy she gave Fagan an unexpected reward, $20.

"No reward," Fagan said before he was able to track down Brooks because for Fagan, keeping the true meaning of the season was his own reward.

More Keys

Not all of Freddy's "key stories" have been as touching or as happy as the one involving Janet. Some have been nothing short of frightening. This is especially true of keys left in unattended motor vehicles.

Joe Fagan recalls a time when they lived in Chattanooga and his father tried to organize a little league football team. Joe was a player, Freddy was the ball boy. On one particular day, it seemed that the ball boy duties weren't providing enough entertainment, so he wondered off. He wandered off to the family vehicle. The keys were in the ignition. He climbed in. He imitated those things he had seen adult drivers do. He started the car. There were no witnesses to the rest of the events. The parking lot was surrounded by upright poles connected with horizontal wire. The car ended up on top of the poles and wire, with the motor running. Freddy was no where to be found. He just walked away. Fortunately, no one was hurt and it is now just one more funny anecdote in a life full of such events.

Don Calhoun remembers a similar incident that occurred in the 1990's. Apparently, some things don't change much. This time it was a bus, or, as Don describes it, "A ratty old bus from the Red Speaks Barn Dance country music show."

The show, a version of the famous Grand Ole Opry show, had rented the Ritz Theatre. The bus was parked on Leinart Street, a road with an incline, not far from the Anderson County Courthouse.

Freddy climbed aboard. He disengaged the brake. The bus rolled across Main Street and came to rest against a building that now houses the law firm of Hunt and Hunt. Again, no one was hurt.

One classic Freddy moment occurred because someone did not use his keys. That incident also took place in the 90's, and it demonstrates how curious and ubiquitous he can be. Just as he checked the doors at Hammers, he apparently checked to see that other places were securely locked as he made his way around HIS town. After all, he has a badge, and handcuffs, and a toy gun.

One night, for reasons passing understanding, he checked a gas pump at a Shell station. The station was closed for the night, but someone had forgotten to secure the gas pump. Almost immediately, as if some secret signal beamed across town, people were lining up to get free gas. Freddy was waving people in, the gas was flowing, and a crowd was gathering. Fortunately for the dealership, the owner was notified and arrived before all of Anderson County could partake in Freddy Fagan's Free Fill Up.

He does have a knack for finding things – for being involved in all kinds of (mis?) adventures. It is a "key" part of his legacy.

A Night in the Life

On October 21, 2010, the Oak Ridge Wildcats visited the Clinton Dragons. It was a rare Thursday night game, part of State Farm's Rivalry Thursday promotion. The game was shown on local T.V. For days leading up to the game, Freddy would meet people and shout, "Ball game."

The words ball game replaced hello, or any other greeting. Its pronunciation wasn't unusual, although sometimes the "lls" were replaced with a "w." Often, the single word was not sufficient, so, "Ball game, ball game" was shouted. And why not, it was the arch rival "Pushycats" who were coming to town. Few things fire him up like football games against Oak Ridge and Anderson County. Once, a local radio station "interviewed" Freddy. According to his brother John, Freddy used that opportunity to say, "Damn Pushycats." It's hard to beat a live broadcast.

On this particular television broadcast, Freddy would be a star. New C.H.S. band director Daniel Stone decided that it was time for Clinton's favorite son to direct the band. Officially. He had been doing it unofficially for decades. It was like authorizing what was already happening, but with a small twist. This time, he would get to use the big platform usually reserved for the drum major. It was a magnanimous and touching gesture, one that thrilled Director Fagan – at least initially.

Freddy took his place as the guest conductor, the band began to play, and all was right with the universe. Then he looked down.

His fear of heights, and falling, overcame him. He was helped down, but the band played on, and the Dragons took the field.

His night was far from over. Mark Packer is a local celebrity. He has his own sports show on WVLT, and does work on the MyVLT network – including the broadcast of the State Farm Game of the Week. His partner in the booth is former U.T. and N.F.L. star Terry Fair. An exchange between these two people demonstrates the far reaching impact of Freddy.

State Farm presents a $1,000 check to the host school during each broadcast. Who was standing on the field, next to Athletic Director Jim Davis and Principal Eric Snider? Who else? He does have a knack for finding the camera. In fact, since he didn't have a check to hold, he was holding the current schedule/poster for the football team – a poster that included his picture. Again. It would be some form of blasphemy if it didn't.

Mr. Packer estimated a viewing audience of 100,000 people for an earlier broadcast. It is unclear how many were watching at the time Freddy was on camera, but anyone who saw it heard Packer say, "Freddy is Mr. Clinton Dragon. He loves the Dragons, and he'll tell you all about them." Mr. Fair added, "And he'll tell you in a colorful, Freddy way."

This was not Packer's first interview with Freddy. A year earlier, during half time of another football game, he interviewed Freddy and Alvin and Casey Taylor. Ever the coach, Alvin had coached Freddy about not cussing on the air. During the interview, Freddy was asked what else he liked besides Dragon football. He replied, "Vols." It happened to be a bad year for the Tennessee Vols, a year that would end with long time Coach Phillip Fulmer being fired. Packer asked Freddy what he thought of this year's team, and Freddy told him, "Coach tink." Packer could only laugh and reply, "And there you have it."

When the interview was over, with Mark Packer still talking on the air, Freddy looked at Alvin, like a kid looking for approval, and asked, "Me good?" He was so good that Alvin's cousin, who lives in Georgia, would call to say he saw the interview on Sports South. The legend continues to grow.

How popular is Freddy? Popular enough that a former N.F.L. star knows about him. Popular enough that one of the best known sports casters in Knoxville knows him. And that wasn't all.

Heather Harrington was there. Ms. Harrington is the popular former Lady Vol volleyball player who now tri-hosts a morning sports talk radio show, covers U.T. football practices, and serves as the sideline reporter for the State Farm games. She has appeared on posters of her own. The statuesque blonde covered another check presentation. Bob and John "Sleepy" Williams were presenting a check on behalf of the Clinton Optimist Club. This time Freddy was there as a presenter. When Harrington said, "Now Freddy, don't take that big check," he responded, "Shoot no." His newest girlfriend felt compelled to repeat it. "Freddy says, 'Shoot no.'" Then she laughed the laugh of another local celebrity charmed by Clinton's honorary band director.

That was the extent of his television exposure, but not the end of the interesting parallel that continues to exist between Freddy and the Clinton 12.

The members of the Clinton 12 were being inducted into the Clinton Wall of Fame during halftime. It was not an accident that the Oak Ridge game was selected. As intense as the rivalry is, there is a wonderful aspect to it. When Clinton High School was destroyed by a bomb – the bigoted reaction to integration – Oak Ridge was the school system that offered classroom space, football equipment, whatever was needed. It was the Oak Ridge band that greeted the displaced Clintonians with the Dragon fight song on the first day. And fifty-four years later, fifty-four year old Freddy was leading the band while the Clinton 12 were receiving a standing ovation, and the media were praising both, and all was right with the world, except that the Pushycats won.

The Ultimate Road Trip

Bob Williams isn't sure how long he has known Freddy. It is somewhere between forty and fifty years. He remembers Freddy at various ball fields, riding a tricycle, chasing after the bike riders. He sees that as a metaphor for Freddy's life – always pushing, always trying to keep up.

Bob and his wife, Bobbie, and their sons, John and Steve, have had numerous "Fredventures." They have taken him to countless high school and college football games, basketball games, and baseball games. They have taken him to the annual Coal Train Days in the Big Stone Gap area of Virginia – a Freddy favorite. But no adventure matches their journey to the home of one of Freddy's favorite professional baseball teams – the Chicago Cubs.

Freddy is basically a Braves fan. He loves doing the chop. He loved John Smoltz, especially when he had a beard. Somehow that made them kindred spirits. When he is pretending to hit a ball, he is Chipper Jones. But Freddy is not afraid to jump on other bandwagons from time to time, especially if the bandwagon goes to Chicago.

John is known to many by his nickname – Sleepy. Sleepy is not an easy word for Freddy to pronounce; it comes out as, "Cree Cree." Cree Cree does the radio broadcast for Clinton High School basketball games. Freddy travels with him to the away games. He tells people, "Me workin'" as he goes through the pass gate. He is never charged. But local trips, or short day trips are one thing. A train ride to the Windy City is something else.

Sleepy's insight into Freddy's personality and popularity would make Will Rogers proud. He states, "Freddy hasn't met anyone he doesn't know." Those words would prove prophetic at the baseball shrine known as Wrigley Field. They rode on Amtrak. During the ride, Bob made one of those seemingly innocuous comments that, like Sleepy's insight into Freddy's personality, would prove prophetic. He said, "I'll bet we see someone who knows Freddy." He wasn't looking for an actual wager, he was simply observing that Freddy's fame transcended Clinton.

They went to the Sears Tower, where Freddy tried to ride an escalator sitting down. This did not go well – ending with a cut leg.

At the ballpark, Freddy wanted a shirt – a ninety dollar Greg Maddux shirt. When it became obvious that neither Bob nor Sleepy was going to purchase it for him, he did what he tries so hard not to do. He spent his own "nunny." He had plenty. He spent it "Freddy style," turning his back so no one could see how much he actually had, grudgingly giving the cashier one twenty dollar bill at a time until he had finally purchased the shirt.

The travelers enjoyed one of the rites of passage that day. They sat in the bleachers at Wrigley. Freddy did something he only does occasionally – he had a beer, an Old Style beer. "His boys," the Cubs won that day. They beat the Brewers 6-2.

When the game was over, the travelers went to the restroom and spent some time locating a misplaced sweatshirt. That's when it happened. Someone was yelling his name. The dulcet tone of "F R E D D Y" was being sung at Wrigley Field. Former C.H.S. student/athlete Michael Zody had traveled from Memphis to Chicago only to find the Clinton icon. Bob Williams would have won his bet. Five hundred miles from home, someone did, indeed, recognize Freddy.

As they were about to leave, they noticed an area where a small crowd had gathered. Curious, they went to see what was happening.

They learned that the Cubs manager, Dusty Baker, was about to appear to sign autographs. When he did, Freddy was there to meet him. How did he react? According to Bob, "Just like he was meeting anyone else." Freddy's comment about Mr. Baker? "My pal," proving Sleepy's point about Freddy not meeting anyone he doesn't know. Or like.

The way the Williams family treats Freddy is not the exception in Clinton, but it is exceptional. What does it say about people who go out of their way to take him to so many places, who treat him like he's just one of the guys, and who relish the opportunity to include him as they would a member of their own family? It says that Freddy is lucky, and so are the Williamses.

Keeping Score

Anyone who spends any time with Freddy will see the comical, whimsical side of him. For Bob Williams, that side is best expressed by a very simple, yet incredibly humorous act. Not surprisingly, the act took place at a Dragon football game.

As Bob recalls, "It was half time, and Freddy was just standing there, arms crossed, looking at the field." What happened next was the kind of unscripted, spontaneous act that is pure Freddy. He strolled out onto the field, somewhere around the twenty yard line. He put down an imaginary ball on an imaginary tee and took a few steps back. He now had the attention of the curious crowd. He proceeded to kick the imaginary ball toward the goal posts. "He kicked the ball, (of course there was no ball), and he kept looking and looking, like he was watching it in flight, and finally, he raised his arm to signal that it was good. Of course, the crowd went crazy."

Freddy had scored again. Years earlier, in 1990, he had also scored, only that time the ball was not imaginary. That time the sport was softball, and Sleepy Williams was involved.

Sleepy's softball team was in Murfreesboro, playing in a Class D softball tournament. Of course Freddy was there. Of course he took "batting practice" with the team. None of that was unusual, in fact the unusual would not occur until the end of the game.

It was the last inning, and Sleepy's team was losing 9 – 2. That's when the right fielder, Mike Cheatwood, made a diving attempt in the outfield and broke his leg in the process. When the inning was over, two immediate problems (in addition to the injury) became apparent. First, the team had no substitutes. They had arrived with just enough players to play. The second problem was that Mike was due up first, and if he could not bat he would be recorded as an automatic out. There was only one solution: Enter the Fredmeister. That's right -- Freddy Fagan would actually bat in a game.

He grabbed a bat and went to the plate – hat pulled way down over his eyes. He swung at the first two pitches, missing badly. Sleepy, on deck, yelled "Pull your hat up." Freddy threw the hat at Sleepy. For reasons known only to the opposing pitcher, the next four pitches missed badly, and Freddy went to first base. There is little doubt that it was an act of compassion, the kind of thing Freddy brings out even in his opponents.

Now Sleepy was up. He loved to hit to right field. The first pitch he hit foul – foul on the first base side. In other words he almost hit Freddy. Freddy yelled, "Cree Cree – 'at way." And he pointed to "that" direction.

Cree Cree hit the next pitch into the gap between right and center and took off running. In his excitement, he forgot who was on base in front of him. As he describes it, "I rounded first and was halfway to second before I looked up. There was Freddy, standing on second base, hands on his hips."

Everyone was yelling for Freddy to keep running. By the time he eventually got going again, the relay throw was being made. A good throw and he would have been out, but this was the charmed Clinton icon running the bases. The throw was so wild that Freddy was able to score. And he did so with a style that only he could muster.

An attractive woman was keeping score behind the home plate area. Freddy had, not surprisingly, noticed her. After he crossed home plate, he did what any superstar athlete/Casanova would do. He blew her a kiss!

Sleepy's team, or perhaps at that point Freddy's team, made a valiant come back that fell short. Freddy was actually waiting on deck for an encore appearance, but it was not meant to be. Of course the outcome pales in significance compared to the glorious moment when The King, the Mayor, Mr. Clinton himself crossed home plate and blew a kiss to the scorekeeper.

In hindsight, it was potentially dangerous. Freddy's reflexes are slow – he would have trouble avoiding a hit or thrown ball. But to coin an NCAA basketball reference, for one shining moment he was a superstar.

Cougars and Courage

The list of people who know and love Freddy would not be complete without the name of Jeff Kidwell. In fact, the entire Kidwell family has become another adoptive family.

Jeff's wife, Connie, (pronounced Ronnie) his youngest son, Brice (pronounced Rice) and his middle son Blake (pronounced Lake) all have a special appreciation for Freddy and his way with words. Even Jeff gets the special treatment. His name is Je (short e – no f's). Only the oldest son, Brad, escapes the "name game," and that's only because Freddy calls him by the number from his baseball jersey. Brad wore number 22, so he is known as "two-two." But no matter what they are called, the Kidwells are all about including Freddy in as many activities as possible. Of course, doing so will, inevitably, create classic moments that are stranger and more humorous than fiction.

Sometimes, the less advance notice Freddy has for an event, the better. The birthday countdown, for example, can last for months. The weeks before the Anderson County Fair are interminable. So the event that would become an "instant classic" didn't have too much build-up, just enough to get Freddy's excitement meter to the frenzied level.

Jeff had arranged an outing. Freddy was, as they say in Clinton, psyched – pumped – wired. And the psyched – pumped – wired Freddy was at the Taylor residence, trying to tell Alvin and Casey why he was so excited. They got the point about his excitement -- that was obvious. But even the almost always reliable Alvin couldn't decipher the cause. Freddy kept saying something that sounded like, "Cougars." Over and over, "Me ready. Me cougars. Me cougars 'night."

The only thing the Taylors could come up with was that nearby Campbell County, nicknamed the Cougars, must be having some sort of activity.

Finally, in a fit of honesty, Alvin admitted, "Freddy, I have no idea what you are talking about."

That's when Freddy held his hands out in front on his chest, making the universal masculine sign for a certain part of the female anatomy, repeating, "Cougars."

Suddenly, it was clear. Trying to suppress fits of laughter, Alvin asked, "Do you mean Hooters?" Are you going to Hooters?"

Freddy's response? "Shoooooot yeah."

And he went. It was a Kidwellean moment – an inspired choice for Freddy's 50th birthday celebration. Even the mayor (the elected one, not the honorary one) would eventually join what would become an annual event.

Jeff has been around Freddy enough to read his moods and the subtle changes that occur. On that first trip to "Cougars," Freddy was feeling like royalty. As Jeff describes it, "He got that swagger going. He walked in, let out a, 'Wahoooo,' and the Hooters girls just loved him." Of course they did. How could they not?

Just like there are DVDs of Freddy at wrestling matches and tapes of him singing *Amazing Grace*, there are photos of him at Hooters. He is a busy man with diverse interests. He even has framed photos of his "Delightfully tacky yet unrefined" girlfriends. He has been known to kiss the photos good-night.

Anyone who has ever taken Freddy to Hooters has witnessed another fascinating idiosyncrasy. When a Hooter's girl waits on a table, she leaves a note with her name on it. Guess who slyly reaches for that note and puts it in his pocket?

With Freddy, for every silly or tacky action, there is an opposite and equally touching reaction. And if Jeff knows the craziness of the Hooters trip, he also knows the courage of fighting cancer. It began as kidney cancer, metastasized to his lungs, adrenal glands, ribs, and his brain. He has had brain surgery. He continues to wage the valiant fight. And he does not hesitate to credit Freddy as being an important part of his recovery, stating, "He is an inspiration to me." It is clear that Jeff wants more time, more ball games, more special moments, and yes, more trips to Hooters. That's really not too much to ask.

See You in Church

Freddy loves church, although his attendance is sporadic. He went often as a child. Numerous friends and relatives have attempted to bring religion to him, and they usually succeed – for a while, and then he seems to lose interest and drift away until the next attempt at redemption.

This is not to imply that he isn't sincere in his efforts. There exists, in several homes in Clinton, a tape of Freddy singing *Amazing Grace*. It may be the most genuine, sincere, off-key rendition of that song known to man. And his presence at the Second Baptist Christmas pageant is one of Clinton's finest traditions.

This is no ordinary pageant. It is a living nativity scene, complete with livestock. Camels have been brought in – and Freddy loves that. He has shown particular affinity for the flatulent nature of the beasts of burden.

Freddy plays a shepherd -- an angelic shepherd who has, at least on one occasion, been wearing a Hooters' shirt under his robe. But even that fashion faux pas pales when compared to another classic church moment. Who else can combine wrestling and religion?

Katherine Miller has taken Freddy to church on many occasions. She is the pianist who accompanied Freddy on his classic version of *Amazing Grace*. And she got to witness one of Freddy's most memorable moments. It happened on a church trip – a trip to a church in Cookville, Tennessee. It would be the trip where the bus stopped at a Shoney's and Freddy sauntered in and announced, "Me back." But it was his performance during the church service that made this trip a classic.

Freddy was seated in the front row of a very lively church – lively in a Fundamentalist sort of way. There was a great deal of activity as the congregation worked itself into a fervor of religious energy. People were feeling the moment, being filled with the spirit. One woman, in the throes of that feeling, rushed to the front and threw herself down on the floor. She lay there, face down, rapt in the moment. That's when Freddy jumped from his pew, went to her side, and in his best imitation of a wrestling referee, announced, "One . . . Two . . . Three . . . You out!"

It is not known how that particular parishioner felt about being counted out in church. It is known that stifled laughter, and some un-stifled laughter, followed.

Freddy's church attendance is not limited to Sunday visits. He is often seen at weddings and funerals – a true testament to his popularity.

The Kidwells made sure he was there for Brad's wedding. When "Two Two" married Brittney, Freddy was dressed up and ready to party. With his jacket and tie and hair slicked back, all Jeff could think of was Carl from the movie *Sling Blade*.

It is always a special moment when the ceremony is completed, when the bride and groom have been introduced for the first time as husband and wife, and they begin their symbolic journey together from the altar to the back of the church. Only Brad and Brittney's journey would have a unique twist. As the newlyweds passed by Freddy, he just couldn't resist. He reached up and gave Old Two Two a high five. It is not traditional. It is typically touching.

Of course the wedding is only half the fun. The reception is where Freddy gets to eat "robsters." It was really shrimp, but he called it lobster – with his own twist on the pronunciation. When Connie helped him loosen his tie, he said, "Ronnie broke my tie."

He was in the front row when Casey Taylor got married, and Don Calhoun is especially fond of a picture perfect moment when his son Kelly got married. It is the proverbial Kodak moment with the groom, the best man (who was also the father), the preacher, and Freddy. In fact, the honor of Freddy's presence is requested at an incredible number of weddings.

Steve Williams requested the honor of Freddy's presence when his daughter Tabitha got married in Jonesborough. At the reception, the every-popular "Kiss Cam" was introduced. When the camera stopped on Freddy, an attractive young woman name Sasha planted a kiss on this cheek. To this day he talks about that kiss. To this day he talks about being mad that he hasn't heard from her.

He is also a presence at funerals. He is genuinely sad and concerned and compassionate. But that doesn't mean he won't have a "Freddy moment," even at a funeral.

Robby and Todd Holbrook played baseball for Alvin Taylor. Their mom, Brenda, was a fixture at the courthouse, and one of Freddy's myriad girlfriends. Her death in 2010 bothered Freddy, so much so, that he called Alvin to say, "My girlfriend die." They talked about it, with Freddy using the word he always uses in such cases – "Shame."

When Alvin asked if he would like to go with him to the funeral, Freddy readily agreed.

Alvin arrived at the appointed hour and his passenger got in. It was dark, and Alvin wasn't really paying attention to Freddy's attire. When they arrived at the funeral home, there was a crowd, people were greeting them, and Alvin still wasn't really paying attention, nor did he until they had moved up in the long receiving line. Then he did pay attention.

Freddy was wearing his Clinton High School baseball pants. And a Hooters' shirt. Doesn't everyone wear that combination to a funeral?

When they reached Robby and Todd, Alvin said about all a person can say; "Here is the only guy who can pull this off."

The Holbrooks understood as Alvin apologized for not inspecting his friend's clothing. It would be unthinkable for someone else to do this. For Freddy, it just adds to the mystique – and the legend. And it is impossible to be upset with someone who is so sincere in his sympathy, even if it does create an amazing visual.

His sincerity makes up for any wardrobe malfunction. When Chuck Miller died, Freddy called his brother Joe. He was crying when he said, "My pal died."

Freddy doesn't always do funerals in baseball pants and Hooters' shirts. In fact, one now defunct funeral home once hired him to help at funerals. They dressed him up and he would pass out programs or do various small jobs during the service. His career in the funeral business was not a lengthy one, but it did end with a bang. Literally.

Freddy had successfully worked at several funerals. But he had never done a military burial, not until one day at a cemetery in Lake City. Apparently, no one felt the need to explain that military funerals come with a twenty-one gun salute. Freddy, who is jumpy and easily startled to begin with, wasn't even looking when the first volley was fired, but a clearly shaken funeral worker screamed, "God damn – me shot!" It was the beginning of the end for his funeral career.

Sometimes his sense of time and place may lead to awkward situations. Sometimes he is inappropriate. But he is always loved. Perhaps no one captured the essence of that juxtaposition better than the valedictorian of the class of 2004.

A Love of Place

Amanda Kay Seals was the valedictorian for the class of 2004. The general theme of her valedictory address was "love of place." In talking about her speech and her town, she offers the following insights:

"I spent a lot of my life in Clinton justifying the idea that I was 'from Clinton.' It can be a very insular place, as I imagine many small towns can, and so somehow the idea that I could consider myself to be 'from Clinton' while my parents were not raised there was incongruous in some minds."

A bright young woman wrestles with her sense of place. How does one define one's home town? For her, the answer was easy. Speaking of Freddy, she says, "He is the salient embodiment of the best things about Clinton for me – the fact that he can go anywhere and someone will always take care of him, feed him lunch, give him clothes, golf clubs (at his city-sponsored birthday party), just about anything else he needs or wants. He brings out the best in people."

A valedictorian addresses her graduating class and talks about Freddy. She observes that, "He brings out the best in people." It is difficult to overstate the significance of such an event. And Freddy's influence on Amanda does not end there.

Amanda had to give a different kind of speech when her father died. As he was at graduation, Freddy was there – and his presence mattered. "I remember looking up from the pulpit at my dad's memorial when I was speaking and seeing Freddy in the crowd and seeing him downtown a few weeks later and him coming to hug me. I am not really even sure how to explain how that made me feel, or if it has anything to do with my speech, but it has everything to do with Freddy. To that extent, I guess it's totally relevant."

A love of place. A person who brings out the best in others. Valedictory addresses are made of such things.

All in the Family

It's 4:00 p.m. on a Friday afternoon. And, thanks to Football Boy Jason Rhodey, Freddy is in the Clinton High School cafeteria taking part in the pre-game meal. He is eating with the other coaches.

He yells, "Cool it, boys" to a table of football players. The reason? Only Freddy knows. The players react with good humor, and the eating continues.

Coach Andy Stattuck is one of the many coaches willing to take care of Freddy. He is welcome at the team meal, he is welcome to ride the team bus, and he is welcome at the annual awards banquet.

Freddy coaches the team and directs the band and still finds time to heckle the officials and boo the opposition. On this night, the very busy celebrity will journey to Campbell County, where his Dragons will prevail, 34 – 21.

It is not surprising that Coach Shattuck is comfortable with Freddy. They have known each other for a long time. And it is quite possible that some of Andy's genuine concern for Freddy is part nature and part nurture.

Andy's father, Jerry, is an attorney and a member of the Clinton City Council. In 1956, he was the President of the C.H.S. Student Council when the school integrated. Jerry's leadership and calming influence are chronicled in the documentary *The Clinton Twelve*. And according to his son, he demonstrated those same qualities as a parent.

The Shattucks lived in the same neighborhood as the Taylors and the Fagans. In fact, they were only three houses away from Freddy. And as early as Andy can remember, Freddy was there – "one of the guys," even though he was more than a decade older.

Freddy was the first mentally challenged person Andy met, and as a child, he was curious. He remembers talking to his parents about it. All these years later, he remembers their message. Freddy is unique and special. He is NOT to be made fun of. Period.

Andy speculates that others in the neighborhood must have gotten the same message, because he and his friends eventually took over the role of protectors. In his circle of friends, it was just not okay for anyone to pick on Freddy. He has an eloquently simple explanation about the neighborhood parents, including his own: "Parents taught decency."

The lessons were well taught. During his high school years, Andy attended many parties where Freddy was an invited guest.

A quarter of a century after Andy graduated from high school, things came full circle for him. He went back at this alma mater, coaching football and teaching history until stepping down in 2011. Freddy called him every night before a football game to remind him that he would be riding the bus with the team. Not that the coach would ever forget. Nor would he forget to have a new shirt waiting for his assistant coach.

Coach Stattuck and his family are part of the on-going love story that is Freddy's story. When he tries to put it all into perspective, the first thing that Andy mentions is how incredibly loyal Freddy is, and the unbridled joy with which he lives his life. He adds, "There is a gentleness to him – an indomitable spirit, and a thirst for living and for life." Coach and Freddy are pals. Always have been. Always will be. Coach knows about loyalty, also. His parents were good teachers.

Father and Son

Casey Taylor played on one of the best baseball teams in Clinton High School history. His father was his coach. The relationship between Alvin and his son is especially close.

After leaving high school, Casey played college ball – first at Walter's State, then at Tusculum College. It was only natural that he follow in his father's footsteps; coaching certainly was part of his D.N.A.

Casey would begin his coaching career at Cocke County High School, and he would ultimately schedule six games against his father.

The father vs. son coaching match-up was so rare in Tennessee high school history that it received considerable attention in the local media. And of course, Freddy would be in the middle of it.

Even though Freddy likes the Braves and the Cubs, he was a fan of Hall of Fame catcher Johnny Bench. Alvin actually helped Freddy write a letter to the Cincinnati star. Of course Bench was long-retired by the time of Casey's coaching debut in 2003. But that didn't matter to Freddy when he made his typically memorable grand entrance at the home of the Fighting Cocks.

Casey had prepared his team. He told them all about Freddy's antics at baseball games. He should know – Casey had been around baseball and Freddy his entire life. The Clinton team bus pulled in, and Freddy was the first to exit. He did so with a war hoop – his best Nature Boy Ric Flair scream. Then he looked at his friend Cray

Cray, clad in the red and white colors of his new school, and with no hesitation yelled, "God damn – Johnny Bench."

So much for introductions and first impressions. And while the word choices may be of questionable appropriateness, there is no questioning his memory or his ability to make appropriate associations. Many years after Johnny Bench quit playing, Freddy was able to remember and associate the Reds uniform with the one Casey was now wearing. And he did so as only he can.

Of course he had to have a Cocke County shirt, and when Casey gave him one that wasn't brand new, he was very upset with that, even if it was the best Casey had to offer.

Freddy's loyalties were challenged. He loves Coach, and the Dragons, but he also loves Cray Cray. He actually spent some time in Casey's dug out, causing several Clinton fans to tease him unmercifully.

The Taylors would do battle until Alvin retired in 2005. That's when Casey returned home to coach his alma mater. Perhaps no one was more relieved than Freddy. For Cray Cray, it would provide an opportunity to be with his pal and assume all of the responsibilities his father had. Those responsibilities require knowledge of logistics, transportation, psychology, meteorology, communication, and interpersonal relationships. Occasionally, some baseball strategy would also be included.

The torch may have been passed, but nothing changed on the Freddy Front. The hits just kept on coming.

Going Green

"Sometime this spring, we will get on a bus and head to Clinton. At some point, one of my players will ask, 'Coach, do you have Freddy's shirt?'" Clark Wormsley was the coach at the Webb School in Knoxville until 2011, and he offered those words before his final season. They reflect on his character, and Freddy's impact on strangers.

Clark's team is called, "Green Shirts," and Clark's name is pronounced, "Cwark." He would not think of coming to Dragonland without a green, Webb Spartan baseball shirt. He adds, "Every player I've coached knows and cares about Freddy."

Perhaps the players are reflecting their coach. Clark has known Freddy since the 70's, since he was a teenager, growing up in Lake City. When he contemplates the Fagan popularity he concludes, "Freddy is so open and real. There is no deception – no hidden agenda. Freddy is always Freddy. He talks to everyone." Isn't that something everyone would like people to say about him or her?

The Webb School has an extraordinary campus with top notch facilities. Before their current baseball stadium was built, the old one was situated right next to a hole at one of the greatest names in golf history – Dead Horse Golf Course. Golfers would hit their tee shots and often have to play their second shot very close to the baseball field. The arrangement provided Freddy with a unique opportunity for entertainment. He would watch the golfers line up their shot, and, just as they began their back swing, he'd yell "Fore" at the top of his lungs. More than one rattled golfer stepped away from his shot, only to hear howls of laughter emanating from the prankster.

Once, in 1999, Webb's coach was recovering from throat surgery. He was hoarse, barely audible. When Freddy heard him trying to speak, he said, "God damn – God damn voice – me coach. You green no."

When Casey Taylor took over as Clinton's coach, he inherited the duty of making sure Freddy was on the team bus for an away game – and he did so, most of the time. But there was a road trip one day, and . . . well . . . the coach forgot. It was a jamboree in Oak Ridge, and Clinton was to play Webb. The coach had myriad duties, things to get ready, and the next thing he knew, he was in Oak Ridge and Freddy wasn't, and Freddy was not about to take such indignity calmly.

When Freddy arrived – he called the usual suspects and got a ride – he immediately let Cray Cray know, "Me mad." He remained mad – walking past the Dragons and into the Webb dugout. When the coaches met at home plate prior to the game, Clark opined an understated, "Buddy – you messed up." All Casey could do was agree, as Freddy sat in the Webb dugout booing the Dragons. He was lip-quivering mad as he yelled, "Leave me, boo. Boo." Then he started yelling at the umpires, who were ready to warn the Spartans until they realized what was happening.

The relationship between the rival coaches epitomizes the way things should be. They compete, they work hard, but they do so with respect for their opponents – and a sense of humor. A sense of humor is a must, especially when Freddy is part of the equation. Nothing proved that more than a classic moment at the Webb School.

The game was over. The two teams had shaken hands and left the field. Clark and Casey were standing at home plate, saying good-bye. Freddy quickly walked past them, heading down the third base line toward the left field corner. The two coaches stood, puzzled, wondering where he was headed.

It is important to note that, because of his medication, Freddy often has moments when he needs to use the bathroom. Immediately. It is also important to note that the Webb School facilities are second to none. Their campus is like that of a small college. Their baseball field is an enclosed, manicured gem.

Apparently, Freddy thought there was a gate in left field – a gate that would provide access to the bathroom. That was not the case, and when Freddy finally realized that he was closed in . . . well . . .

There really was only one solution – and fortunately most of the players and fans had left, but two amazed rival coaches watched what happened next. It is hoped and believed that Freddy is the only person to pee in left field at the most exclusive, private school in East Tennessee. Some rivalries are just more colorful than others.

"Ball Game, Ball Game"

It is impossible to overstate the impact that sports have played in Freddy's life. And it is impossible to overstate the impact Freddy has had on the area coaches.

Tom Froning has coached Oak Ridge baseball for thirteen years. He looks forward to playing Clinton because of the rivalry, but also because of Freddy. "He is definitely one of the first people I look for when we play them." He adds an interesting insight into their relationship by adding, "I try to antagonize him when I get there."

Initially, such an admission might sound harsh, but it is actually the ultimate sign of affection. Freddy loves to tease and to be teased. He understands that Tom is kidding. And he loves to give it back.

Tom is known as Pussycat Coach – or Damn Pussycat Coach – it just depends. He has, on more than one occasion, fired a baseball into a chain link fence or backstop when Freddy was passing by, just to startle him. Freddy is not afraid to yell at the perpetrator of such dastardly deeds. Froning adds, "He has a special relationship with all of the other coaches." It is clear that Freddy has touched the Pussycats' coach.

He also touched another rival coach – almost literally. Bud Bales coached Central High School to an undefeated state championship in 1990. Current Colorado Rockies star Todd Helton was on that team, and Todd and his coach had a close encounter of the Freddy kind.

Bud's name, in Freddy World, is Bug. Todd is Bud's boy – or Bug's boy. Their encounter occurred during Freddy's "golf stage" – a period where Freddy felt compelled to travel with a golf club – ala Bob Hope on a U.S.O. tour.

The setting was Fountain City Park. Alvin Taylor and "Bug" were talking. Todd was nearby – getting ready to play. Bud forgot the promised shirt and hat, and was explaining that to Freddy. Next thing the Hall of Fame coach knew, Freddy was approaching, the golf club was between his legs, and Freddy was lifting it upward – up toward a place where golf clubs were never meant to be. Coach Bales moved quickly enough to avoid any "discomfort." Coach Taylor testifies that Bud's boy was laughing hysterically. Two decades later, that close encounter can still produce gales of laughter.

Freddy did not get a Central shirt and hat that day, but he did eventually get a Central letterman's jacket. As Central rolled to a championship, Freddy jumped on their bandwagon. He likes a winner. Fast forward to 2008. The University of Tennessee is retiring Todd's number. It is a huge deal for Todd, the university, and the community. There is a banquet at the Knoxville Convention Center, and all the local dignitaries are there.

Casey Taylor was there with his father Alvin, and Jim Payne and Don Calhoun and Don's son Kelly. And Freddy.

When the Clinton delegation arrived, they discovered what Casey describes as an incredibly long line – a line of people waiting to see Todd – to get an autograph, or a picture, or just to shake his hand and congratulate him. It was a jacket and tie affair for many in attendance – with one notable exception.

Freddy was not in a jacket and tie. Since he was going to see Bud's boy, and Bud's boy was a Central High School alum, he wore the most logical item of clothing he owned – a Central letterman's jacket that, by this time, had become what Casey describes as, "Old and ratty." Under the jacket he wore an <u>old</u> Clinton High School shirt. Certainly, one does not forsake his team completely. The outfit was completed with one of Freddy's favorite items – his white baseball pants.

Freddy not only failed to conform to the fashion norms, he flaunted the conventional approach to waiting in line. Freddy weaved his way in and out of the well-groomed movers and shakers until he was right next to Todd's table. Todd was in the process of signing an autograph when he heard, "My boy."

Todd looked up and yelled, "FREDDY!" And that's the way it is – time after time in Freddy World. He moves to the head of the class – or the front of the line – listening to the beat of his own drummer, following his own "fashion sense." In the process, he connects with people. Todd Helton was college baseball's player of the year. He is an all-star, a millionaire, and a celebrity. He is also a fan of Freddy Fagan. Casey describes Todd as genuinely happy to see him. That speaks volumes for Todd – and for Freddy's ability to touch lives. This time, he left the golf club at home.

Hoskins

It is a landmark, a local treasure, and an institution. It is a gathering place, a place where nostalgia permeates every aspect on the business, and it is another "Freddy place." The official name is Hoskins Drug Store, but it, like its iconic visitor, has become a single-named entity. To the locals, it is simply Hoskins.

Stepping into Hoskins is like stepping back in time. It has the feel and charm of a 1950's malt shop. That is by design. It has a long lunch counter with red, padded stools, an old time soda fountain, and milkshakes made the old fashion way – in large, silver containers that contain more than a glass worth of milkshake. There are numbered booths, and there are more than a few regulars who have "their booth." The wood in some of the booths has messages carved in it. The walls are full of pictures from the early days of the store.

In 2010, the store celebrated its 80th anniversary. They cooked over 800 hamburgers that day. Freddy was there. In fact, it is hard to imagine any major celebration happening without his presence.

Hoskins is today what it was when it opened more than eight decades ago – a family owned and operated business. It began in 1930, when the late R.C. Hoskins, and his late wife, Katherine, opened the original store on Market Street. In 1947, they opened the store on Main Street. The original site is now Hoskins Medical Supplies. It and the drug store are the only sites still in operation, but at one time there were thirteen such stores in East Tennessee, including one that is now the site of another famous landmark – Big Ed's Pizza in Oak Ridge.

R.C. and Katherine had four daughters – Sheree, Kathy, Dudley, and Mollie. The latter two are the current co-owners. And the family operation does not end with them. Dudley married prominent banker Jenks Bostic. Their two daughters, Mollie and Jenky, both work there – making them the third generation to do so. Jenky was a basketball player at Clinton High School. She was best known for her three-point shooting ability. It is a tribute to Freddy's memory that, even though she graduated in 1993, whenever Freddy sees her he makes a shooting motion and says, "Three points."

Jenky and Mollie were managers for the baseball team. Mollie recalls a time when they were getting ready for a team picture. Freddy was there – it isn't an official team photo if he isn't in it. As the photographer was getting ready, Freddy told everyone to say, "Cheese." Only it didn't come out as cheese. It came out as, "Chee," as in, "Say Chee." Mollie admits that, to this day, whenever any thought of any photo occurs, one of them will invariably utter, "Say Chee," and both of them will laugh.

The Hoskins family grew up across the street from the Fagans. The Fagan sisters were, and continue to be, close friends. They remember playing dress-up – and including Freddy in the process. They remember Dr. Bishop teaching the neighborhood kids to ride their bikes. Dudley remembers Freddy riding well – but not doing such a great job of stopping. She remembers him zooming down the road and into a garage without applying the brakes. He crashed into the back wall, and got up holding a specific part of the male anatomy. Not that he would be deterred from riding.

The Main Street location is perfect for many reasons. The store is across the street from the courthouse, next door to the Ritz Theatre, and the back of the store is visible from Freddy's Place – The Towers. He can see (and yell at) Dudley when she empties the trash. He can watch to see who might be walking towards Hoskins. Of course, being so close, Freddy is there often.

Mollie Hoskins Scarbrough gives a great insight into the character and the personality of Clinton's favorite son. It began in October, when she casually mentioned something about Hoskins getting a Christmas tree for the store -- and asking if he might want one for his apartment. Of course he did. Mollie had counted on that. What she didn't count on was the daily inquisition about the tree. Day after day, she was greeted with some variation of, "My tree here? My tree ready?"

Eventually, some time after Thanksgiving, the tree arrived. When Freddy found out, he went to stand by his tree – and he remained there, guarding his tree, until someone took it to his apartment. If the tree had been there all day, Freddy would have been there, also. There is no telling what would have happened if it had remained there over night.

After growing up in the same neighborhood, after seeing him so often at work, it is not surprising that the Hoskins family and all of their employees have a special fondness for him. Kayla DeMarcus is typical of many Clintonians. She loves his smile, his energy, his happiness. The six year Hoskins employee also loves how he yells across the parking lot at her, and how he gets "mad" at her if she is with her boyfriend. Perhaps Dudley says it best: "We all take a little ownership in raising him." Maybe that "ownership" explains why, as Mollie describes it, "Freddy is pictured in every Hoskins wedding. It is just expected that he will be there." Somebody probably told them to, "Say chee."

Fairy Tales and Dragonland

When Katherine Hoskins passed away, the town turned out in force. The fire department and the police department escorted the hearse from the funeral home to the cemetery. People lined the streets – creating a parade route of sorts. And there, in the front, standing reverently at attention, was Freddy. Mollie and Dudley still become emotional as they recall the basic, eloquent humanity expressed in that simple gesture. Once again, Freddy touches hearts.

Still, for every touching action, there is an equal and opposite tacky reaction. In March of 2011, *The Sports Animal,* a sports talk A.M. radio show, broadcast live from Hoskins. Not on the air, fortunately, but in front of the broadcasters, Freddy addressed Mollie Scarbrough about her recent trip to the beach. He said, "You beach?" However, it did not sound exactly that way. Fortunately, Mollie is trained in Fredspeech, but for those who weren't, the conversation sounded as follows:

Freddy: You bitch?
Mollie: That's right – I went to the beach.

One has to wonder what people unfamiliar with Freddy think. Of course, the Knoxville broadcasters know Freddy, and when he informed host Josh Ward that there was a book being written about him, Josh announced it on his show. Months before the book was close to being finished, Freddy was already promoting it.

For every tacky or inappropriate-sounding action, there is an equal and opposite touching reaction. Natalie Scarbrough knows, and thanks to her efforts, so do her classmates at the Webb School.

Maybe it's because Natalie's mom has been so close to Freddy for so long, or maybe it's because her dad is Clinton City Police Chief Rick Scarbrough, and the chief is vigilant in his attempts to watch out for him, but whatever the reason, Natalie is another descendent of the Hoskin family who has been touched by Freddy.

Natalie is very much a "Clinton girl," even though she is a graduate of the Webb School in Knoxville. During her senior year, she was honored by her selection to give a speech that is known as Chapel Talk. Hers is a speech about growing up and accepting change – about roots and values and rites of passage. And it is a speech about the love affair between Freddy Fagan and Clinton, Tennessee.

Natalie begins with a metaphor – a metaphor rooted in the magic of fairy tales. She selects Shrek as the archetype of her quest. She leaves the metaphorical swamp of Clinton for the Land of Far Away that is Knoxville. Even the loveable Donkey has a role. Like Amanda Seals before her, she finds herself contemplating a sense of place. And, like Amanda, she finds Freddy to be an intricate, perhaps even quintessential embodiment of what she holds dear to her.

Her words sparkle with the insight of someone who knows and loves her town. "My Shrek Fairy Tale would not be complete without a fun-loving Donkey always there to brighten the day. If any of you have ever been to a Clinton event of any kind, you have probably seen Freddy. Freddy was born with mental retardation, but has never let that slow him down or break his spirits. It is often said that the entire city has helped raise Freddy at some point. He lives for Dragon sports, and is no doubt their number one fan. He goes to every home and away game he can get a ride to, and is most likely the loudest one in the gym. Some of you may have even seen him at a Webb game. After a year of convincing, he finally agreed to put on his 'green shirt' as he calls it, and come watch the Spartans. No matter how far away I journey from the swamp, I know that Freddy and everyone else will be right there waiting for me when I get back."

How successful was Natalie's speech? When it was over, the President of the Upper School (Webb's term for the older students) congratulated her and expressed his desire to meet Freddy. Such is the magic and power of words – and of Freddy.

Natalie's reference to the green shirt is, of course, typical. Shirts are always important – and Freddy's trip to watch Natalie play basketball for the Spartans required the appropriate shirt. Freddy showed up at Hoskins properly attired and raring to go. Unfortunately, he was a day early. Fortunately, his enthusiasm would last for twenty-four hours, and he would make his appearance with typical fanfare.

Natalie concludes her speech by acknowledging that neither Clinton nor Knoxville are perfect, but that she is lucky to have found the best of both worlds. She adds that the overwhelming lesson of the fairy tale is, ". . . Things never turn out the way they seem, but they always turn out right . . . That is my happily ever after."

Freddy and Shrek and the Webb School and great speeches and a sense of place. Is there a better recipe for happily ever after?

HEP ME! HEP ME!

Hammers is not just a bargain discount store. It is an institution. The reasons for its lofty status are varied, but they include its role as a gathering place, a place to keep up with local current events, a place to stop and socialize and save money. It is also a place that has employed a multitude of people from Anderson County, and while the quantity of people hired is impressive, the quality of the employees is amazing.

For years, Margaret Calhoun taught English at Clinton High School. She was in a unique position to hire excellent part time workers. Even after she left teaching to work full time at the store, the legacy of students who worked at Hammers during high school and/or college, then found successful careers is extraordinary. Numerous doctors and lawyers and teachers and business leaders all have resumes that include working at Hammers; and that experience often includes rich memories of Freddy.

The experiences of Cynthia Bridges are representative of that group. Cynthia is an Anderson County High School graduate who spent four years at Hammers beginning in 1993. Even though she was "a Bull," the rivalry did not stop her from becoming one of Freddy's favorite girlfriends. The remarkable aspect of their relationship is that, to this day, Freddy is not sure of her name. He knows it if someone talks about his girlfriend Cynthia, but ask him her name and he may go blank. In fact, Cynthia will sometimes ask just to watch him squirm and quickly change the subject. But while he may not know her as Cynthia, he knows her as a girl whose company he loves – as someone who genuinely cares about him. She also had her share of Fredventures, like the following:

"A few of us at Hammers watched Days of Our Lives during our lunch breaks. Since I watched it, Freddy started watching it with me every day and got into it. On days I couldn't take lunch at that time and had to miss it, Freddy would watch for me in the break room and come out during commercial breaks to update all of us in the basement. I still remember one update vividly. The character Marlena had been buried alive by the evil Stefano. They kept showing internal coffin shots of her fighting for her life. Freddy's update: 'At one gurrl . . . HEP ME! HEP ME!!' The 'help me' was in a high falsetto voice.

"It's been years since I've watched it and I remember next to nothing about the plot lines from fifteen years ago – but I remember that one!"

Cynthia graduated from Roanoke College in Virginia. Sometimes during college breaks she would work at Freddy's favorite store. She has two more classic Freddy experiences.

The first happened about twelve or thirteen years ago, when Cynthia went to visit Freddy at his place. She knocked on the door. She heard, "Come in." She started in, but quickly realized Freddy had just gotten out of the shower. He was naked. A quick turn, and a hastily uttered, "Go get dressed" was all that was required to rectify an embarrassing situation. It is a visual that will stick with a person, although a short time later they were talking and laughing as fully clothed boyfriend and girlfriend. Freddy would hold and stroke her hand, and rest his head on her shoulder.

The other experience involved yet another wedding. Freddy's role in this one is unique and unbelievable – even by his lofty standards.

April Hunley was getting married to Jason Giles. Cynthia had a date for her friend's wedding. She was being escorted by Mr. Fagan. It was a natural. She wouldn't have it any other way. During those times when she was dating someone, Freddy would get extremely jealous. She laughs as she recalls how one male friend had the audacity to rub her shoulders in his presence. That was not okay in Freddy World, and he made sure everyone knew it. To this day, he gets lip quivering mad if she mentions the incident.

Once, Hammers received two rings from the Q.V.C. network. Don gave one to Freddy, who re-gifted it for a special occasion. Cynthia still has the ring and the Valentine card that came with it.

The day of the Hunley/Giles wedding, Freddy was the epitome of sartorial splendor. He was once again an important fixture at another Clinton ceremony. Only this time he would provide a memory unlike any other.

Prior to the wedding, Jason suffered a broken leg in a farm accident. He was limited in his mobility. The traditional first dance with the bride and groom was in jeopardy. Enter THE stand in. The lucky bride had a first dance for the ages. April and Freddy – dancing. It is special. Unique. Touching. But it is not unusual. Time after time he finds his way into an event. Time after time he finds a way to leave his mark on that event. The fact that it does, indeed, happen time after time proves the point that the extraordinary is to be expected; it is what usually happens.

April and Freddy danced. They danced to a song from the movie *Grease*. They danced to *Freddy My Love*. It was a once in lifetime dance with a once in a lifetime partner. *Freddy My Love*, indeed.

The Dark Side

"If Freddy shaved his head it would be a mess of scars." With those words, Joe Fagan reveals part of the painful side that is his brother's life. Joe should know. He has watched his brother receive myriad stitches from myriad injuries. Fortunately, Freddy has an incredible threshold for pain.

Joe recalls being with him once when he had to have staples removed. Normally, this wouldn't be a huge ordeal, but this time one of the staples had turned. The doctor couldn't get it without digging for it. Freddy never flinched – never needed the offered anesthetic. When it was over, the doctor remarked, "I have never seen anything like this before." Of course, that statement is true on so many levels where Freddy is concerned.

As a child, Freddy had a habit of walking with his hands in his pockets. This did not help his balance, and he fell often. Later, he rode his bike. This was a time long before the now common sense practice of wearing a helmet. More injuries occurred.

Once, Freddy fell at Clinton Middle School. He was bleeding, in need of stitches. An ambulance was called. Mollie Scarbrough found out and called her friend – Freddy's sister, Donna. Mollie followed the ambulance to Oak Ridge Hospital. At some point, Freddy noticed her and started waving. He was hurt and bleeding, but still smiling and waving to his friend.

There were other falls and ambulance rides – one happened years earlier outside of Hammers, the other happened years later outside The Towers, when he broke his hip. But not all of Freddy's scars are physical.

There are those, in all towns, who are predators, who have NO qualms about taking advantage of someone like Freddy. The city and county police have done an admirable job of watching over him. Chief Scarbrough remembers being a young patrolman and picking him up as he was walking or hitchhiking to various events. He says, "There are police all over, not just in Clinton, who know Freddy." He also agrees with the comments of Freddy's sister Donna, who says, "There will always be people who pick on people like Freddy."

He has been robbed several times, the most recent being in 2010 when he lost $75.00, or as Freddy says, a 5-0 (fifty) and a 2-0 (twenty) and a five. Freddy was the person who called the police. And there are other predators as well.

Like any small town, rumors abound in Clinton. There are rumors about people who tried to get Freddy to smoke or drink or take drugs. There are rumors about people of little character engaging women with less than stellar reputations to perform intimate acts with Freddy. For Joe Fagan, one rumor proved true. It was an incident with a remarkable twist.

It was 2000, or maybe 2001, Joe's not sure. It was night. There was a knock at his door. A man he vaguely recognized, an acquaintance, stood there. He was there because he was concerned about Freddy. There were a few guys with marijuana, hanging out on the streets. Freddy was with them. He wanted Joe to know.

Joe called the police. He's not sure which officers responded, but he knows what they did. They could not prove any wrong doing, but they could close the area as a place to hang out. They could promise the men that anything that endangered Freddy was a serious mistake. They could ask Freddy if he wanted to go to jail. He didn't, but the message had been sent.

When Freddy's mom found out, she was justifiably angry. When she confronted Freddy, he told her, "Me quit. Me church."

That was that. Certainly Freddy does not smoke or do drugs now. It wouldn't be much of a story, except that there are always a few degrees of separation between Freddy and bigger events.

Joe states that the man on the porch – the one he vaguely knew, was Mark Foster, and if his name wasn't, or isn't, a familiar name in Clinton, his actions are. About a decade after he showed his concern for Freddy, a disgruntled fourth grade teacher was told he would not be rehired at his school. The school was Inskip Elementary School. One February afternoon in 2010, that teacher shot the principal, Elisa Luna, and the assistant principal, Amy Bruce. They would survive and eventually have an emotional return to their school. Mark Foster, the man who wanted no one to harm Freddy, would be arrested for attempted murder.

There are other rumors; rumors that are difficult to verify. Most of them are not the type of thing people readily admit to, and if it were confirmed, what would it matter? It would only serve to prove what is already known, that a few people with bad intentions and evil motives exist, but that their significance pales when compared to the many with good intentions and pure motives.

Still, the negative experiences in Freddy's life have left their marks. The lack of fatherly affection cut deeply, and the entire community was deeply hurt by an act of brutality inflicted on him.

It was the 70's, and Budweiser beer and radio station WOKI sponsored a river raft race on the Clinch River. The Clinch runs through Clinton, and the event attracted thousands from all over East Tennessee. There are few details of what happened. It is doubtful that any local resident witnessed the attack because someone would have stopped it, or reported it, or revenged it. Freddy was beaten. Severely. He was found bloodied and dazed and unable to provide much information about the perpetrator. There seems to be a consensus among his relatives about what most likely happened, but there are no eyewitnesses besides Freddy, and his ability to detail the exact sequence of events is limited.

The best guess is that someone from out of town, most likely under the influence of alcohol, beat Freddy because he called the wrong person his girlfriend. Of course "wrong" in this case is from the point of view of a person who obviously felt it was "right" to beat up someone with no ability to defend himself.

Clearly, this was a low point. But sometimes the purpose of a low point is to provide a springboard for reaching higher points. In a way, Freddy was lucky. There was no lasting physical damage. It is hard to detect any lasting psychological damage. It certainly did not stop him from attending future social events. It did not stop him from being his usual, gregarious persona. It did not stop him from flirting and using the word girlfriend.

In the tradition of the very best love stories, good triumphs over evil. Those who would attempt to lead Freddy astray might have a temporary, short term success, but ultimately, they would fail. Freddy does not smoke or do drugs, and he will only rarely drink a beer. His moral compass is remarkably good. And even the most vile and sinister pariah cannot beat the enthusiasm and joy out of Freddy. The town won't allow it, and Freddy won't allow it, because that's how love stories work.

Elements of Style

For years, Freddy made "the rounds." He still does, but the rounds have changed dramatically – partially because Freddy is older and slower, and partially because some of his favorite places are no longer within walking distance. In addition to places that have closed, like the White Store and Twins Café, some have moved. The Mexican Restaurant, Los Caballeros, has relocated. So has Little China. The day Hammers relocated was one of the darkest days in Freddy's world. He told Don how mad he was at him. According to his brother John, he stood on the sidewalk, staring at the empty building where he spent so much time, just shaking his head.

Fortunately, there is still the Apple Blossom Café and Hoskins Drug Store, and one important new place for Freddy to visit.

For twenty-two years, Marcus Mitchell has owned and run Mitchell's salon and spa. In 2005, he moved his business to Market Street – to a perfect location on the Fagan circuit. Doing so would change lives.

It looks like any other hair salon, but as is often the case, things are not always what they seem, especially when Freddy is involved. And Freddy is certainly involved with the entire Mitchell family.

Just like Hoskins and Hammers, Mitchells is a family business. Marcus and his wife Tiffany and their daughter Alexa all work there. On weekends, youngest daughter Hannah does, also. And once the business was established in Freddyland, it was only a matter of time before they became the official stylists for the "mayor" of Clinton.

Marcus recalls seeing Freddy around, but they hadn't really had much interaction. "He just walked in one day." That's all it took. The Mitchells made him feel comfortable, Freddy charmed them, and just like in a classic black and white movie, it was the beginning of a beautiful relationship. Freddy began to come in more frequently, and once he felt relaxed, he began to be . . . well . . . himself, complete with loudness and teasing and more frequent appearances.

Just like Freddy gets free food and free clothes and free movies, the Mitchells found a way to join the list of those who contribute to his well being. They wash his hair, cut and style it, and dye it if he requests it.

Now, Freddy stops in three or four times a week. He'll yell at someone, "Go to work." If someone is missing he'll accuse them of shattin' 'round. He'll have a snack, talk about what is going on in Dragonland, or just sit and relax. Of course he flirts with some of the customers. If his hygiene is lacking, it will be taken care of. But the real fun begins when he has "stylistic concerns."

Sometimes, Freddy has a beard. When it is neat and trimmed, odds are he has visited Mitchells. Sometimes, Freddy has highlights in his hair, compliments of Mitchells. He has even had the orange and black colors of HIS Dragons in his beard – and countless other hair colors. Marcus says the orange and black beard was Freddy's idea – that he felt it would impress his girlfriends – a.k.a. the Clinton High School cheerleaders. He was right.

Football Fridays and Freddy at Mitchells is one of those magical small town traditions. Even if he is not due for a "styling," he will usually stop -- in even if it is just to yell, "Ball game, ball game." Of course there are other rounds to make before the team meal, and the band directing, and the coaching.

Sometimes he goes to the Mitchell's house, where son Dylan joins the rest of the family for a pre-game meal. Tiffany recalls a time when one afternoon featured the music of Eddy Van Halen – cranked up loud as Freddy played some air guitar. The Mitchells have seven cats and four dogs. And while the impromptu concert made the dogs nervous, especially Hannah's Shih Tzu, Tiffany makes an interesting observation about Freddy and her pets. "He is great with the dogs. They don't bark at him." It's almost as if they know better, or sense his uniqueness.

A family business changes location -- and the ripple from that movement creates a Butterfly Effect of the Freddy variety. Yet another Clinton family learns the joy of his company. He becomes a part of their family – they willingly take him places and care for him. The Mitchells are giving him free grooming and meals and attention, but they are gaining far more. They look forward to his visits, to his ability to entertain customers, and to the joy he spreads.

Marcus speaks for his entire family, and maybe the larger family of Freddy's friends when he talks about why he enjoys being with him. He observes, "It's because he's real, because he is honest, he is always the same, there is no mask."

How much better would society be if everyone fit that description? It is clearly another example of a special needs person teaching the so-called "normal" people a valuable lesson. Clearly, the Mitchells are willing to listen and learn.

Mom and son

Dad and son

The baby in Germany

Joe (left) and Freddy

From left - Freddy, Joe,
Angela, and Donna

Camping in New Jersey
Front Row: Freddy, Joe, Angela, & Donna
Back Row: Freddy Sr. & Barbara

Chipped tooth from a pillow
fight with Joe and Dad

Family

Talking Dragon baseball are Clinton fixtures <u>Alvin Taylor</u>, Freddie Fagan and Jeff Kidwell.

With permission from the Clinton Courier

Getting the sign from the catcher

Casey Taylor and Freddy - 1997
District Champs
(note who holds the trophy)

Christmas with Alvin and Casey Taylor

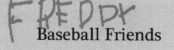

Baseball Friends

"Ball game, ball game"

Relaxing

Gatlinburg - early 2000's

"You out"

FREDDY
The Boy Wonder

Freddy, Alvin, and more than three decades

FREDDY
With Alvin Taylor

Freddy and Don Calhoun at Hammer's

Sleepy, Freddy, and Bob

With Baby Buck - Julia Payne

Dudley, Freddy, and Mollie

John's girl, Margaret, and the boy wonder

Bye Ran and Freddy

Freddy's personal stylist, Marcus Mitchell

Friends Around Town

A Hoskin's milkshake

His 50th birthday present

The 2011 Dragon's baseball team

Cray Cray and his assistant coach

The key to Freddy's place

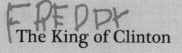

FREDDY
The King of Clinton

Donna, Barbara, Freddy, John, and Angela - 2011.

Freddy and John

The house on Eagle Bend

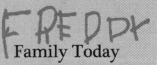

Family Today

The door to Freddy's place

Some of the 1,200 shirts

Kicking back at the Chief's desk while Mrs. Hammer is away

John Schmoltz in action

Free movies at the Ritz

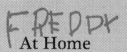

FREDDY At Home

The approach   The kick

The flight   Crowd goes wild

Good again

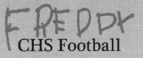

CHS Football

Amy Kidwell, Freddy, Lindsey Lane

Clinton High School football game on September 9,
2011. Madison Fritts, Courtney Fritts, Freddy,
Savannah Fritts, and Hunter Crisp

Cynthia Bridges and Freddy at
Hammer's - 1993

Cristine Trivette, Patty Shoemaker, Freddy,
Lisa Smith.

Katherine Birkbeck and Freddy - 1999

Leisa Burton with Freddy at JC Park - 1975

FREDDY **Girlfriends**

The Pranksters

Freddy loves to tease people. He loves jokes and pranks and laughing his unbridled laugh. He also loves being the "victim," although he will give the impression that he doesn't. No matter how mad he swears he is, on some level he understands that teasing is a sign of affection.

He has hidden inside a box elder with Alvin Taylor, armed with a hose, waiting to soak unsuspecting Halloween pranksters. That was years ago, but to this day, if he is asked if he remembers Alvin and the hose, he will grin that broad grin and nod his head and say, "Shooot yeah."

He was with Alvin when some pranksters were intent on rolling the Taylor's property with toilet paper. The pranksters made a critical mistake. They left their keys in the car, and the coach and his assistant snuck around to the cars and confiscated the keys. The pranksters enjoyed rolling the yard, at least until they discovered they could not leave the scene of their crime. It was a classic case of he who laughs last laughs best. Or in Freddy's words, "Me, me – you keys."

The visual of Alvin and Freddy, prankster partners lurking in the night, is as rich as an image can get. Imagine how it must feel to be foiled by Freddy.

The street that bears Freddy's name leads to the Apple Blossom Café. One day, Webb Coach Clark Wormsley was eating there with several friends, including Freddy. This was shortly after the official dedication of Freddy Fagan Way, and Clark was doing what comes naturally -- he was teasing the man for whom the street was named. He complimented him on a fine looking sign before casually adding, "I just might have to take that when I leave."

The exact response to such a "threat" isn't remembered now. Odds are excellent that it was either, "Bull, no," or some kind of "no" invoking a higher power, or perhaps a verbal assault mentioning the word punk. Clark really didn't give it much thought, nor did he think much about it when, a few minutes later, Freddy left. In fact, the entire episode might have been forgotten if not for one poignant aspect. When Clark left the Apple Blossom, he looked toward the street sign. There was Freddy, standing next to it, guarding his legacy. "Old green shirt" was not getting that sign.

Todd Helton is not just a great baseball player. He proved to be a first class prankster as well. It was the district tournament, and Karns High School was the host. Clinton was there, and so was Todd's Central High School team. Somehow, when Central finished their game, Todd and his teammates were able to sneak Freddy onto the Central bus. They hid him in the back until the bus pulled out and headed home, at which point Freddy stood up to address Coach Bales. "Hey Coach. Me hungry. We stop." The bus turned around, the "kidnapping" was forgiven, and Central won a state championship, but not without some laugh-until-you-ache moments on a team bus heading home.

There are those who prank call Freddy, and those he tries to prank – although it is not hard for anyone to figure who is calling when he is on the other line. But the master of the prank – the ultimate, the guru, the grand pooh-bah of pushing Freddy's buttons is Dennis Pratt.

The Button Pusher

It is the 1980's, and the boom box is the rage. So of course Freddy has one. This was back in a time where he would frequent Clinton's pool halls. Yes, he can play pool. He was in his 30's, and fit, and he was seen all over town carrying his boom box.

Once, Bob Williams asked him, "Hey, do you have some good music there?" The response was Freddy's garbled equivalent of, "No batteries."

Just because a boom box doesn't have batteries is no reason to leave it home – and someone would surely rectify that problem.

Once he had batteries, there was still the issue of the tape he had. It was blank. At least it was until Dennis Pratt realized what was happening.

From 1980 – 1988, Dennis worked at the Clinton Hammers. He went to the Maynardville branch for a while, and now he runs the store in Sevierville, and if anyone loves to push Freddy's buttons, he is that person. And a boom box with a blank tape is way too much for Dennis to resist. It is a blank canvas that needs his artistic touch.

Dennis recorded a tape – a tape of insults. He called Freddy a big fat ape. He said that Freddy wore girls' underwear. It was a litany of comments he knew would anger his target. A little distraction, a placing of the tape, an off-hand comment from Don Calhoun about there being something in his boom box, and . . . Viola! Instant chaos.

Almost three decades later, Dennis still laughs about it – and not just about the initial reaction. For the next two weeks, Freddy went around playing the tape for different people. And as Dennis remembers it, "He'd get mad, but he kept playing it. He'd rewind it and then get mad all over again." Of course that is exactly what he wanted.

Dennis decided to be Freddy's nemesis – the person he loved to hate. It was not mean-spirited, and Freddy certainly was a willing participant, but those who worked there, such as twins Josh and Caleb Tipton, readily agree it was a constant barrage.

The Tiptons even helped perpetuate a Dennis classic. They all told Freddy that Christmas was cancelled one year. Denials and curse words not-withstanding, the verdict was in: No Christmas. It was events like that which led to the name Freddy has for Dennis: Punk Ryin' Jennon, which is translated as Punk Lyin' Dennis.

The countdown to Freddy's birthday assumes epic proportions. It begins about forty-eight hours after his last birthday ends, although it doesn't really surface until after Christmas. In February of 2011, he was talking about the upcoming birthday, saying things like, "Five – Five," and holding up five fingers on his right hand twice so people would know he was going to be fifty-five. Sometimes he'd add, "Me old."

This is not a new thing. When Dennis worked at Hammers, Freddy would come in and point to May 30th on their calendar and remind people of the monumental event coming soon. This happened for years, until Dennis took the situation (and some scissors) into his own hands. He cut out the date of Freddy's birthday – just left a gaping hole there. When the day came to turn from April to May, when it was time for the future birthday boy to point to his day, there was nothing to point to. Freddy was talking, laughing, pointing when . . . the realization that something was not quite right slowly seeped in, followed by his, "Hold a minute."

Freddy stared, repeating, "Hold a minute." That's when Dennis felt obligated to explain. With a straight face and Punk Ryin' Jennonillian logic, he calmly explained that the President had declared May 30th an illegal day, and that anyone born on that day could no longer have a birthday. That triggered responses that are hard to adequately capture in words. Some of them start with the word, "Bull." Some begin with certain references to a higher power. Some simply start with, "No," perhaps followed by various and sundry cuss words. Sometimes the response begins with, "Punk Ryin' Jennon" before morphing into other insults, including – but not limited to – "Dumb Dumb." "You out," might be heard. But the exact response was not important. The goal was to get a response, and when Dennis was finished, the mission was accomplished.

It got to the point that just the thought of Dennis would make Freddy mad – but still he came back for more. Capitalizing of his love of wrestling, Dennis would couch his comments in the best (or worse) wrestling terms. They would "fake wrestle." They would talk trash to each other. Sometimes the wrestling wasn't entirely fake, not when Nature Boy Fagan got riled up.

Dennis doesn't get to see Freddy these days, and he clearly misses that. The Tipton twins still see him around town, and Josh offers an amazing insight into the uniqueness that is Freddy. As identical twins, they were constantly being confused for the other twin – except by Freddy. Josh states, "He never once mixed us up. He always knew – he always called us by the correct name." He truly never ceases to amaze.

Call Me

Freddy has a cell phone. That fact brings a smile to many faces in Clinton. The manner in which he uses that phone brings a smile to many more.

Freddy keeps the phone in his pocket, and even though he receives numerous phone calls daily, he always seems surprised when his tropical ring tone sounds. Of course, he tends to be jumpy anyway, and the ringing phone invariably startles him. Once he has gotten over the surprise, he has to fish for the phone. Depending on which pocket of which item of clothing the phone is in, this may take some time. He occasionally misses calls while he is fishing, although he is very quick to return one once he has retrieved the phone.

The standard greeting does not change. He can be counted on to respond to an incoming call with one word: "Yeah." The word may be loud, it may be drawn out to last longer than most one word responses, but it will be one word none-the-less. And even though he has no caller I.D., he is incredibly quick at discerning who is calling him, even if the caller doesn't immediately identify himself or herself.

People have been known to prank call him. During Halloween, Sleepy Williams will play a long, ghoulish laugh which has been known to cause Freddy to imitate the laugh in a sarcastic manner before saying, "Shut up, punk."

Freddy is perpetually looking forward to the next holiday, and the next big event. The day after Halloween is over, it is time to get ready for Thanksgiving. And few things capture the holiday spirit like a recorded message from Clinton royalty.

Freddy's messages are unique when they don't relate to the holidays. Just as he always answers the same way, he is fairly consistent when he is the caller. Usually, he just starts talking – no social amenities or small talk gets in his way. If he is talking to an answering machine, he usually begins with the word, "Hey," followed by a name and the message. He will often end with, "Call me." There are many people who have messages on their cell phone that will never be erased. The messages are quintessentially Freddy, and funny. But when the holiday spirit is added, the messages are instant classics.

Sleepy Williams has a classic Thanksgiving message. It begins, predictably, "Hey Cree Cree." It continues with Freddy's best (?) imitation of a turkey gobble, a rather lengthy gobble at that, followed by the consistent ending, "Call me."

Don Calhoun has a Christmas message for the ages. It captures Freddy's love and joy of the season, his appreciation for Don's tradition of allowing Freddy to walk through Hammers and select items that people will ultimately purchase for him, and a vintage moment all in one. It begins, "Hey, John, Ho, Ho, Ho, Santa Claus comin' to town . . . you, me, store . . ." And then he belches. There is a pause, and then, "Me sorry. Call me." After Christmas (or Chris Chris) there is the reminder to Alvin to buy Bye Ran a Valentine rose, and then it's time to get excited about the beginning of baseball season and Easter. In 2010, the Cell Phone King dressed in an Easter Bunny costume to help with the Clinton Optimist Easter Egg Hunt. He had actually done it once before, and the suit was hot, so he refused to do it again. That is, he refused until money was offered. Freddy in a pink bunny suit -- too good to be true.

Then it's time to talk about his birthday, and the fair, and football season. And every day, 365 days a year, the cell phone works overtime. He has memorized the programmed numbers for those he calls daily. It is an impressive list.

He talks to his two brothers daily, and other family members as needed. Don Calhoun and Sleepy Williams usually hear from him, and pals like Jeff Kidwell just never know when the most unique voice in town will be heard. For Alvin Taylor, the question is usually not if Freddy will call, but how many times. And since time does not really matter to Freddy, some of those he phones have gotten calls at less than desirable times. It is a small price to pay for the honor of being on "his list." And even those not on the list are likely to get a call if a "need" arises.

"Needs" often arise when one or more friends are with Freddy and someone's name comes up. This is especially true if someone's name comes up because he/she has made the Cell Phone King (C.P.K.) mad. The conversation with a Freddy Friend (F.F.) might be:

C.P.K.: I mad.
F.F.: You're mad?
C.P.K.: Shoot yeah, I mad.
F.F.: Who are you mad at?
C.P.K.: I mad damn. . . (fill in the blank with this month's/weeks/ day's/hour's culprit – labeled X for the purpose of this conversation).
F.F.: Why are you mad at X?
C.P.K.: [Actually, C.P.K.'s answer doesn't matter – any reason will do].
F.F.: Well, maybe we should call X – what do you think?
C.P.K.: [Insert favorite cuss word/words here followed by Yeah].
F.F.: Okay – followed by dialing.
C.P.K.: Hey, X. I mad you. You [insert crime here]. Call me.

And so it goes. Another citizen has "a collectible" -- a voice message that will be played and replayed to countless friends and relatives. A voice mail from Freddy is a status symbol, a badge of honor, and a valued possession. As the saying goes, "Ya gotta love it."

The Stair Way

He was a character – the type of character found in many small towns. He was colorful. He liked to party. He loved his bass boat, and fishing, and Norris Lake. He loved to sing. He enjoyed his beer. And he loved Freddy, and Freddy loved him.

His name was Gilbert Stair, but his nickname was as colorful as he was. He was Foozie to all who knew him, a nickname his father had given him as a child.

In 2005, Foozie passed away. As he had done earlier when Chuck Miller died, Freddy once again called his brother Joe and tearfully repeated his simple yet eloquent tribute – "My pal die." Often the word die comes out, "Guy," but no matter how it is pronounced, it is remarkably poignant when Freddy is forced to deal with it.

Foozie's widow, Sally, has literally known Freddy since the day he was born. In fact, when Freddy was born, Sally was a senior at Clinton High School – the class of '56; the year of the Clinton 12. More than half a century later, Freddy still refers to her the only way he has ever referred to her. He calls her, "My girl."

Today, the place Foozie worked is simply called ACE – or ACE Hardware, but "back in the day," this Market Street landmark was known as ACE T.V. Hardware, and when Foozie worked there, Freddy would visit every day. Sometimes Foozie would put Freddy to work, moving boxes or doing other small chores, and he would pay him. It is noteworthy that many of the most important people in Freddy's life are male role models who gave him a job to do – be it working with Don Calhoun at Hammers, or Alvin Taylor at the pool and the ball field, or Foozie at the hardware store.

Sally is left to tell the stories, a task she clearly relishes. And after 48 years of marriage, she has stories. The mere mention of Freddy and Foozie and the bass boat brings a smile to her face. Of course, Freddy and Foozie and a bass boat sounds like a country song, and that is somehow appropriate, since Freddy loves country music, and Foozie loved to play it. Close family friend Carolin Lefevers says, "Foozie sang Willie Nelson songs better than Willie Nelson."

The two country crooners would venture to Andersonville boat dock for a trip to the Loyston Sea area of Norris Lake. Ostensibly, they were going fishing, but Sally suspects there was a lot more riding around than actual fishing going on. Sometimes, Freddy would drive the bass boat, a visual image too rich for words. Apparently, the refrain, "Straighten it out" was frequently repeated. Sadly, it is a potential YouTube sensation that will never be seen.

On one trip, the bass boat experienced some minor engine problems. Eventually, Foozie would fix the problem, but not before a classic diagnosis from Freddy. His analysis of the situation was typically succinct: "Boat broke."

Clearly, Freddy has many unique qualities and idiosyncrasies. One such characteristic is his perception that situations and events will repeat themselves – that what happened at one gathering will happen exactly the same way at the next gathering. That explains his reason for not returning to Oak Ridge after he was berated by an umpire. In his mind, the next time he went to Oak Ridge the same umpire would be there to react the same way when Freddy yelled, "Strike." Eventually, the perception corrects itself, but it does exist, and it may explain the reasons for a potentially life threatening situation.

Foozie had Wednesdays off. He and Freddy had gone to the lake on Wednesday. The following Wednesday, Foozie stopped by ACE T.V. Hardware for a moment before leaving to go about his business. The lake was not part of his itinerary that day, but Sally suspects it may have been part of Freddy's thinking – i.e., we went to the lake when Foozie was off last Wednesday, therefore, we should be going to the lake this week as well.

Foozie did not know Freddy was down the street walking toward the hardware store. He got in his car and drove off. Freddy saw that and apparently sensed he was being left behind, so he started to run, as if he might catch the departing vehicle. His singular focus was on catching Foozie, a focus that caused him to dash into the road – and into the path of an approaching car. Freddy was struck, and hurt, but once again he dodged any lasting injuries.

Sally does not remember who was driving the car that hit him. She does remember that Foozie felt terrible about the situation, even though he had no way of knowing what was going to happen. All he knew was his pal was hurt, and that was sadder than any country song.

Fortunately, there would be more boat trips, and more music, and more memories. Especially the memories. For Sally, and for Freddy, it is the memories that make that all important connection to a colorful, fun-loving, powerful influence on both of their lives. Freddy smiles when he remembers Foozie. That's what pals do for a person, even after they die.

The Tennis Match

Don Calhoun and Alvin Taylor should co-host a weekly radio and/or television show. The title could be . . . oh . . . any number of things – *Travels with Freddy* or *The Freddy Hour* or *The Life and Times of Clinton's Mayor* or *The You/Me Pals Show*. The possibilities are endless. But they should have the show.

They could tell stories, have a weekly guest like Sleepy Williams or Jeff Kidwell or Marcus Mitchell or any member of Freddy's army of fans, and they could highlight the girlfriend of the week, and each episode could end with Freddy himself holding court on the issue(s) of the day. It would be vastly superior to some of the things that pass these days for entertainment – especially the so-called reality shows.

Until they get their show, local groups should hire them to entertain – to regale the audience with their legendary tales. It would be like watching a tennis match – an hysterically funny tennis match.

The two tennis players would warm-up by repeating some already detailed classics. Don might open serve with the beloved Tea Good story. Alvin might return the serve with the Lawn Mower at Midnight tale. Don could lob over the Free Gas at the Shell Station classic, and Alvin would counter with the Concession Stand Locksmith caper. Once the players were warmed up, it would be time for some fresh stories to fly.

Don would rare back and retrieve one of his golden oldies. It involves an ill-fated delivery to a local trophy store.

It began not long after the town of Clinton had installed new street lights – attractive street lights – expensive street lights. It seems that the driver of the delivery truck did what drivers of such trucks have always done when they have to back their truck into a tight situation – he stopped a man on the street and asked if he would help guide him into the space he was trying to enter.

Of course he had no way of knowing that he was about to become another player in the life and times of Freddy Fagan. He just asked for help, and Freddy did his best.

When it was over, the flustered driver said all he really heard was, "Come on back." Of course, that was not the way it was pronounced. "C'mon back" is more likely, but "Mon back" may be better still. Whatever the pronunciation, the driver came on back until his truck met one of the new street lights. The truck won. The driver was not happy. His helper suddenly remembered that he was needed somewhere else. The talents of Sherlock Holmes were not required to piece together what happened. Instant classic.

Now Alvin would have to serve up a story. No problem. His story would begin, "Once upon a time, there was a sporting goods/pawn shop across the street from Hammers." In fact, there were many places in Clinton whose location was pin-pointed by their proximity to Hammers. And being in close proximity to Hammers greatly enhanced the probability that the mayor would visit as he made his rounds. So it was on the day the glass got cracked.

Like many small shops, this one had items on display that were housed in typical glass display counters. And sometimes glass cracks. Usually, it is an accident, as it was when Freddy cracked it. The owners knew it was an accident, and they weren't really upset. They were kidding when they told him he would have to pay for it. It might have been a non-story – an insignificant incident, except that when Freddy is involved, it is rarely insignificant.

Someone at the store decided it would be funny to prank call him and demand payment. Even that might have been a short-lived moment of amusement had it not been for a classic Freddy reaction. He answered his phone, and when he realized who was calling, and why, he ended the conversation as only he can. He emphatically informed the would-be pranksters, "Me home no." Then he hung up. Those three little words have achieved a sort of immortality in Dragonland.

Don would laugh and acknowledge the beauty of the well-played story. He'd ask, "Remember the wrestling match, when one of the wrestlers had a manager who didn't weigh very much and, as part of the act, he got picked up and turned upside down?"

Alvin would smile and nod affirmatively, knowing the punch line before Don could finish. "So the manager gets turned upside down and all of his change falls out of his pockets, and guess who scurries over and collects it all?"

After a few moments passed — moments dedicated to laughing and recollecting and visualizing the wrestler and the upside down manager and Freddy and the "nunny," Alvin would ask, "Remember when Freddy got Coach Lockard a technical foul?"

It would be Don's turn to smile, as his friend finished the story of how Freddy, sitting on the Dragon's bench, said something derogatory about an official as he ran by. The ref was positive that long-time coach Don Lockard had said it and gave him the "T." The coach was quite capable of getting his own technical, but Freddy helped him that time. Alvin might even digress and remind his partner that, when Don Lockard retired, his son Chris became the coach. Immediately Freddy was ready with a name for the new leader. Since Chris was replacing his father, it was only natural that he be dubbed, "Baby Coach." After twelve years in that position, the coach is now in his early 40's. It does not matter — nor will it matter if he coaches another twenty years. He will always be "Baby Coach" to Freddy.

After a brief message from their sponsor (hopefully an iced tea company) the guest of the week might be ready. Perhaps Steve and Samantha Clapp would be there to tell of the time when they had a party at Jaycee Park for their daughter Laura's fifth birthday. This was over a decade ago, but they still remember the then 44-year-old who happened to walk by and decided that this looked like the place to be.

Of course he joined the party. Of course he was welcome. Of course he had the first two hot dogs. And the first piece of cake. And he fit right in with the five-year-olds, just like he would with people his own age, or with people at a senior citizen's home. He made the party more memorable.

After another commercial – this one featuring Freddy selling hot dogs (pronounced dot dogs) it would be time to feature the girlfriend of the week. That would be a highly competitive spot, but this week's selection is a highly competitive person. She is University of Tennessee Lady Vol star Glory Johnson.

Glory and Freddy found themselves in the same Knoxville gym. Freddy was there because the Dragons were there, and Glory was there to see a relative who was playing. Glory is a tall, photogenic woman with a vivacious personality. She was a star basketball and track athlete at the Webb School, and is a captain for the most successful women's basketball program in college history. Her presence caused a commotion. Freddy lives for commotions, and when he noticed Glory, he pointed to her and asked, "Big Orange?"

Jim Davis verified that she was, indeed, part of the Big Orange Nation, and he took Freddy to meet her. When Jim informed Glory that Freddy would like a picture and an autograph, the gregarious Lady Vol said, "Come on up." When Jim informed her of Freddy's difficulty climbing the bleachers, she did not hesitate. She simply said, "Well, I guess I'd better come down." She did, and she was exactly what a Tennessee fan would want and expect a Lady Vol to be – friendly, gracious, and classy. Of course, that is what Freddy's girlfriends should be as well.

The show would end with Freddy talking about baseball, and his birthday, and dot dogs. Time would be up for that week, but the two tennis players would be back the following week with more stories, another girlfriend, and a new feature – the Freddy Fagan Impersonation Contest.

The ratings would be through the roof, but Jody Wright would win the contest.

The Wright Way

A traveler from Knoxville will enter Clinton by way of Route 25W – Clinton Highway. He or she will cross the landmark green bridge. It is really the Honorable William Everett Lewallen Bridge, but to the locals, it is the green bridge. Route 25W will magically morph into Main Street, and many of Freddy's favorite places are within walking distance of Main Street.

If a person did not stop, he or she would quickly be back on Route 25W heading into the "metropolis" of Lake City. The most recent internet listing for the population of Lake City is 1,856 people. Yet this small community plays a large role in Tennessee history and in Freddy's life.

Originally called Coal Creek, Lake City is known for an 1891 labor dispute known as the Coal Creek War, and for the Fraterville Mine disaster of 1902. It is also known for producing successful coaches. In fact, four Lake City natives have coached state championship teams.

In 1987, Shelly Sexton played on Pat Summitt's first national championship team. She is a member of the Lady Vols Hall of Fame. She coached the Webb School women to a state championship. She even coached Freddy's girlfriend, Glory Johnson.

Wade Mitchell and Clark Wormsley have won state championships in baseball for the Webb School. And then there is Jody Wright.

Jody has won two state championships in basketball for

Knoxville's Fulton High School. His teams have been runners-up two other times. He points out that Clark and Wade grew up in the same neighborhood, as did he and Shelly. He and Clark have been friends for most of their lives. Both of them have known Freddy for most of that time. And when it comes to imitating Freddy – an act done frequently in Clinton – Jody Wright is in a class by himself. Nobody does it better.

Jody's grandmother lived in Freddy's neighborhood – across the street from the Hoskins family. Jody would spend much of his summer visiting her, going to the Jaycee Pool, and being around Freddy. His voice inflections, timing, word choice, mannerisms, and overall delivery are perfect.

Jody has another unique "claim to fame." He may be the leader in the nickname category. When Freddy gives a nickname, it tends to stick. He usually dubs his subject with one name. Jody hit the trifecta.

People who have a beard are often called, "Billy Goat." There is a logic to it. Current C.H.S. assistant principal and athletic director Mike Harmening has been Billy Goat for decades. Even when the beard is gone, he is still Billy Goat. Jody has never had a beard, but that doesn't stop Freddy from calling him Billy Goat. Jody has no idea why.

His second nickname does make sense. Jody has, on occasion, been guilty of using smokeless tobacco. When Freddy found out about that, "Chewy Chewy Boy" became the moniker of choice.

The third nickname is another puzzler. If Jody had been born in Oak Ridge, or grown up there, or coached there, "Pussy Cat Boy" might make sense. He did none of those things, but he still got the nickname.

Since Jody's teams often make a deep run in the tournament, they are often the only local team still playing. That means Freddy will end up following the Fulton Falcons. Sleepy Williams is the main provider of transportation. The two pals will journey to the games, and it won't take Jody long to know of Freddy's presence. A 2011 tournament story is typical. Jody recalls that after the game, the media wanted his attention. He actually dealt with them before meeting with his team.

After addressing both of those concerns, he had one more obligation. He knew Freddy would be patiently waiting, and he knew life would be better if the coach came bearing gifts – or at least a gift. Jody met Freddy with a Fulton shirt in hand. He adds, "I have tremendous respect for people like Alvin and Casey Taylor. Coaches have so much on their minds before and after games, and Freddy is a big responsibility, but they always take care of him.

Andy Shattuck would agree. After the 2011 football game at Karns, Andy had little time to celebrate a big victory. Freddy had traveled on the team bus to the game, but the team was ready to ride home, and Freddy was missing. A series of hasty phone calls – a telephone tree of sorts, tracked down Freddy, comfortably riding home with Jeff Kidwell. Only then could the coach relax.

Jody adds two classic stories to the collection. The first is back in the day when Lake City had its own high school. Today, those students would attend Anderson County High, but when Jody was in school he was a Lake City Laker. He can't remember what level of competition was involved (i.e. – freshman, junior varsity or varsity). He just remembers being on a football team that beat Freddy's Dragons. Before the game, he heard a certain local celebrity boo the Lakers, telling them that the Dragons were number one. After the game, when all the players had gotten on the bus, Freddy walked on. He folded his arms and closed his eyes, lowering his head. He held up an arm – the universal sign for quiet – and the bus got quiet. What post game insights did this Bear Bryant, Joe Paterno, Alanzo Stagg persona have to offer? With perfect timing, he told his rapt audience, "Lakers number one." He promptly left to a thunderous ovation.

Jody's second story serves as a reminder that Freddy is very jumpy and easily startled. It began innocently enough. Freddy was walking down Market Street carrying two "to go" cups of Coke. Jody did what many would do. He honked at Freddy. It was meant as a friendly gesture. Only Freddy jumped, and the Cokes went flying, and Freddy got wet. Jody didn't know that part – a witness would tell him after the fact. What he did know was that looking back in his rearview mirror, he saw Freddy standing in the middle of the Market Street, with both middle fingers raised.

Jody enjoys Freddy (middle finger salutes not-withstanding). He enjoys watching Fulton fans react to him. He points out that often someone will hear him or see him and ask, "Who's that?" Someone will answer, "Oh, that's Freddy," and the questioner will nod. Even people who don't know him know of him, and just saying the first name is identifying enough. The person will just nod that, "Oh, I see – it is all so clear now" nod and life goes on.

Jody received one of the finest tributes a coach can receive; the gym at Fulton High School was named for him. It was a wonderful way to honor his remarkable success. Standing behind the bench, somehow sensing the solemnity of the occasion was Freddy Fagan.

Jody also knows that Freddy innately senses who is laughing with him and who is laughing at him. He marvels at Freddy's instincts and Clinton's pride in what he has accomplished. Not bad for a Billy Goat, Chewy Chewy, Pussy Cat Boy – who is also the master imitator.

Uncle Chewie

Freddy's reference to Jody Wright as Chewy Chewy Boy is interesting and ironic, since variations of that phrasing have been used to describe him.

It is also interesting to note that, of all his titles and nicknames, one of the most meaningful is Uncle Freddy. Uncle Freddy has four nieces and two nephews. Most of them are adults.

Chuck and Donna's oldest daughter, Bekah, has been responsible for two classic Freddyisms, one of which occurred before her birth. When Donna was pregnant, that was the term everyone used – Donna is pregnant. Freddy heard it, and seemed to understand. His sister was pregnant. No big deal, at least not until someone mentioned that she was going to have a baby. Suddenly, it was a big deal, a huge deal. Donna was going to have a baby! She may have been pregnant for some time – but apparently that didn't register. Having a baby did register – and Freddy was excited. Of course, Freddy has always had a tender, affectionate side, especially with children. His siblings talk fondly of how nervous and worried he was the night his mother went to the hospital to deliver John. He paced all night. The dog got nervous enough to start barking thanks to Freddy's anxiety.

Bekah's second moment would happen almost two decades later, when she decided that going to college was no longer what she wanted to do. While her parents are fine with her decision now, there was some initial disappointment, artfully expressed by Uncle

Freddy. His classic assessment, as expressed to his sister was, "B.B. – Chuck pissed off. Bekah school out."

Three years after Bekah's birth, Daniel was born, and three years after that, Hannah entered Uncle Freddy's world.

Murray and Katie Fagan are Joe and Meggie's adult children. Katie observes, "Murray and I could never get away with anything because if Freddy saw us somewhere, he would always call dad and tell him what we were doing." When he is talking to Joe, it is always, "Your boy" if he is talking about Murray, and, "Your baby girl" if he is talking about Katie.

Murray played baseball for the Dragons. The biggest fan of C.H.S. baseball had another reason to be excited about baseball. Uncle Freddy could not have been happier.

Freddy's two brothers sometimes call him Chewy. Katie says it is because Freddy has a habit of "chewing" on his lip when he gets angry.

The youngest niece is, "John's girl," or, "My John's girl." She is Gwenyth, an adorable nine-year-old who clearly loves Uncle Freddy. She remembers being with him at Myrtle Beach, and she is excited when he attends her softball games. Perhaps it is the wisdom of youth that allows her to speak for all of the nieces and nephews. When asked about Uncle Freddy, she simply but eloquently says, "The whole town is his friend."

Some of those friends in town gave Freddy the third variation on the word chewy. This time it does not refer to his lip or to chewing tobacco. And it is spelled differently. It is because of the movie *Star Wars,* or more accurately, a character from that movie. The character is Chewbacca, also known as Chewie. All it took was for someone to point out that there was a resemblance between Chewie and Freddy, especially when Freddy has a beard and long hair, and that was it. The man who is an uncle, the mayor, and the king, would also be known as Chewie.

These days it is not used frequently. Occasionally someone will mention it, but there was a time when Chewie references were quite common in Clinton. And why not? Chewie is depicted as gentle, strong, and loyal. That sounds just like Uncle Freddy.

Mr. Ambassador

Freddy goes through phases. There was a cowboy phase, where he dressed the part down to his trusty cap gun and holster. There was also a cop phase, complete with the requisite regalia. There was the referee phase, and there continues to be a baseball phase. These phases don't completely vanish. They may be abandoned for a while, rejected for new and improved fashion statements. But suddenly, for no apparent reason, the cowboy phase or the cop phase is resurrected again.

A phase seems to require "gear." Some of his "looks" are not as elaborate as the full blown phase, but they are interesting. Often, it only requires a shirt. One example would be his *Star Trek* look. It was during that period of time when yet another special memory transpired. This time the recipients of a little Freddy magic weren't from Clinton.

The year was 2004. Kim and Jim Suiter had heard numerous stories about Freddy. They were close friends of Donna, but they had never actually met her brother. But when their son Wesley, a basketball player for Bradley Central High School, had a game at Clinton, they were determined to see Freddy in action. Kim tells the story:

"Upon arriving in the gym, we immediately started to look for Freddy. We finally asked someone if they would point us in his direction. They gave us an exact location and told us to look for the guy in his *Star Trek* uniform."

The Suiters found him as the teams were finishing their warm-ups. She continues, "We approached Freddy and told him we were friends with Donna and Chuck. He immediately smiled and gave us a hug. Upon telling him that our son Wes was playing for the opposing team, he immediately changed his opinion of us and started giving us the thumbs down with a loud, 'Boo.' After convincing him that Wes was a good guy, Freddy asked which player he was.

"By then, my son's team had gone into the pre-game huddle. The players were talking with their coach on the opposite end of the gym. When we pointed out our son, Freddy made a beeline for Wes. He ran straight across the gym floor. When he got to the huddle, he gave our son a great big bear hug. Our son was quite surprised by this unexpected visitor, but after a quick explanation as to who Freddy was, the whole team welcomed him with high fives and slaps on the back."

Kim adds two lines that are suitable for framing: "It is a memory I will never forget. Clinton should be proud to have such a special ambassador."

To the titles of uncle and king and mayor, add that of special ambassador. It is a most fitting moniker.

The Suiters' experience is typical. Many people know of Freddy. They have heard about him, even though they have never met him. His reputation truly precedes him. Then they meet him, and even if the meeting is a brief one, it may produce lasting impressions – inspiring impressions – life affirming impressions.

His impact is not just for Clinton residents. Local radio station WYSH broadcaster Jim Harris is the voice of Clinton football and basketball. He points out that when Clinton travels to Knoxville Central, their house announcer pays a special tribute to Freddy. He introduces Clinton's starting five, then he introduces Freddy – who promptly rolls out the ball to center court. It is the basketball equivalent of throwing out the first pitch. It is a classy gesture – one worthy of a special ambassador.

Apple Blossom Time

Sometimes Freddy enters the Apple Blossom Café at 9:30 in the morning. That may not seem noteworthy, but it is an hour-and-a-half before the restaurant opens.

There are days when he enters at 9:30 and stays until he has finished his third and final meal, sometime after five. Those are slow days, when there is no game or other activity. Sometimes he is too tired to make the rounds, so he sits and socializes.

When the Millers sold their restaurant to the Hudsons, they included a clause that Freddy would continue to eat for free. When the Hudsons sold the café, there was no such clause included. It was not needed.

Current manager Jane Treece illustrates the point with an anecdote from her first week on the job. An unnamed customer finished his meal and went to pay. As he did so, he casually asked Jane what she thought of Freddy. Jane responded, "He's very special." She indicated he was always welcome there.

The customer smiled and replied, "Good answer. If you had responded any other way, I would never have eaten here again."

Jane had passed her test, and another example of the loyalty people feel for Freddy was revealed. As Jane explains it, "We bought him with the place."

Of course, all relationships have their moments – their proverbial trials and tribulations. Jane estimates that her trial came, "About three or four summers ago." The usually non-aggressive Freddy had a very rare temper tantrum -- in the restaurant. It is likely that a recent change in his medication for a hiatal hernia may have been a factor, but Freddy lost control and over-turned a table. He was shaking. Joe was called and he restored order. He made Freddy apologize and then he banished Freddy from the café. He was told, "You cannot go back in there until school starts." The start of the school was weeks away – almost a life sentence in Freddy's mind. He had not acted that way before, and would not do it again. There were days when he stood on the sidewalk, staring at the restaurant. But he did not enter until school started.

When he did enter, he told her, "Me no mad you Jane. Me like you."

Once again, all was right with the universe. "Jane's" was no longer off limits. They would only have one other minor skirmish. Jane got after Freddy about his hygiene and banished him until he cleaned up. This time there was no yelling or turning over a table. Freddy just told Jane that, if he could not be in her restaurant, she could not walk on his street. It is important to note that both parties now freely frequent the other's prized namesake.

The Freddy Express often charges through the Apple Blossom Café. Jane observes that out-of-towners are initially taken aback. She says that those who have been shopping at the antique malls and stop in for lunch don't always know what to make of Freddy. But then they see the firemen, or the policemen stop by and high five him, and the other customers speak to him, and eventually it becomes clear that there is something special happening here.

Jane also points out that he truly belongs to the town, and the town truly watches out for him. She notes that one time Freddy had his wrestling belt – the W.C.W. one – stolen. She says, "The cops had it back in two hours."

The Apple Blossom is not just a restaurant. It is a gathering place. Sometimes it serves as a place to drop off birthday presents or Christmas presents. Sometimes it's Freddy's public forum. But most days, it is a place to eat and socialize and catch up on the latest happenings in Clinton. Those "happenings" include the latest exploits of the man whose street leads to "Jane's." With any luck, the man himself will be there – sitting at HIS table – the one in the far left corner. He is such a fixture there that someone made a large banner proclaiming it "Freddy's Place." Eventually, it was taken down. The owners got tired of checks being made out to Freddy's Place. But it is an easy and logical mistake to make. It does seem like he owns the place. And why not? He seems to own the rest of the town.

Driving Mr. Fagan

Freddy has a driver's license. Sort of. At first glance it does look like a standard issue motor vehicle license. Closer inspection reveals that it is not the same. The actual license is held horizontally -- with the photo on the left side. Freddy's license is held vertically -- with his photo at the top. It clearly states that it is for identification purposes only, but that doesn't stop him from showing his license.

The "license" was especially handy for boarding a train to watch the Cubs play. It is just one more detail, one more nuance that adds color to the portrait that is Freddy.

Of course he doesn't drive, but driving with Freddy as a passenger is often a "trip" in itself. It begins with one simple rule: Freddy rides in the front. Period. Standard "shotgun" rules do not apply. He will wear his seatbelt, but he does not like to be reminded to "buckle up." However, he has no problem reminding the driver to fasten his or her seatbelt if he or she is slow in doing so.

Even if he is riding on a team bus, Freddy sits in the front with the other coaches. Some of his greatest observations and deepest philosophical moments occur while riding around town. Former band director Tim Paul knows about those moments. He and his staff were riding in Tim's van after an away game at Anderson County High School. Freddy was with them. He says:

"As a staff, we were fairly quiet on the way home. We were analyzing the night's performance and were preoccupied with the fact that we had an early morning the next day. We were leaving at 5:00 a.m. to take the

band to a national competition. Our minds were understandably focused on the next day. As we were driving down Seivers Boulevard, we passed the Kentucky Fried Chicken. It had recently been announced that KFC was closing and there was to be a Walgreens in its place. As we passed KFC in our silence, we hear Freddy say solemnly 'Bye, Bye Chicken House.' I almost ran into the Burger King sign."

Freddy would repeat that phrase often. Once he realized he could get a laugh, he was not afraid to keep using it.

That is the beauty of "Travels with Freddy." There is simply no telling what he will notice, what he will say, or what association he will make. It is almost a stream of consciousness exercise. It is never dull – especially now that he is talking to God.

Baseball weather in Tennessee is problematic at best. Weather conditions change almost as often as Freddy wants a shirt. And his concern over the weather has led him to discuss the issue with God.

Both Coach Taylors have observed this relatively new phenomenon. Casey laughs at how often Freddy takes credit for nice weather. He likes to say, "See – me right 'gain," as if he had been the chief meteorologist for the National Weather Service and had predicted the beautiful day. He might add, "Me God pals." Somehow, bad weather gets no mention from the weather guru.

Sometimes Casey will approach Freddy first and say, "Look how nice it is. You were right." That is usually met with some variation of the always popular, "Shooot yeah."

Alvin likes to tease the divinely inspired weatherman. If Freddy calls on a sunny day to gloat about his meteorological expertise, Alvin may inform him that it is raining where the Coach is. Freddy will respond, "You ryein', Coach."

Freddy has been known to roll down a window and make noises like he is honking a horn if traffic slows things too much. He notices every "cool cat" car, and most cars that have pretty girls in them. He has been known to yell, "Hot momma" out of the car window. He once rode by a bar that advertised topless waitresses, dismissing it with the words,

"God damn titty bar." He misses little. His powers of observation are amazing, his word choice . . . it is amazing as well.

These days, driving with Freddy sometimes means fast and frequent stops because of his need to use the bathroom. It is especially "interesting" when a team bus has to suddenly pullover. He may need help getting in and out of a vehicle. All of this has to be done safely but quickly.

Travel with Freddy also involves food. At some point, a road trip will include a meal, sometimes several meals. And if riding with the King is a trip, dining with him is an outer-worldly adventure. It is not a fast process.

Freddy does not like the drive-thru. He does not like to eat in a moving vehicle. Part of that is because of the difficulty he has controlling things with one strong arm. Part of it may be his social instincts. He was made to be in a crowd. Also, there is no bathroom at the drive-thru.

He has surprisingly good table manners – although he is not afraid to yell if:

a)   He recognizes someone on the other side of the restaurant.

b)   Someone is out with one of his girlfriends.

c)   He feels like it.

He is a wonderful dining companion. In fact, he is like he is everywhere else – funny, uninhibited, and talkative. Occasionally, he does need help, especially if there is food in his beard. Then it is back to the car, or truck, or bus, and on to the next adventure. Hopefully, Freddy has arranged for good weather.

Fredcabulary – Part II

When it comes to girlfriends, Freddy is an equal opportunity ladies' man. He has girlfriends of all possible descriptions, but it is always interesting if his girlfriend has blonde hair. That is because in Freddy World, blonde is pronounced, "bronde."

For years, Freddy was a fan of a certain clown who had his own T.V. show. For most people, that clown's name was Bozo. For Freddy, he was Bo Bo the Crown. He also likes the Three Stooges, pronounced "Doo Doos."

Like many Big Orange supporters, Freddy was a fan of former Tennessee basketball coach Bruce Pearl. Bruce is pronounced, "Roose."

When Kevin Weaver joined Casey Taylor on the baseball coaching staff, he had to be properly initiated. In his case, initiation meant getting a proper name. It did not take long. Kevin shaves his head, so he was formally dubbed, "Bald boy."

Freddy does an amazing thing with the words, "cell phone." For most people, those words are accented on the first word. Freddy is somehow able to accent both words equally. His inflection is similar to what he does with the word, "girlfriend;" his voice rises like he is asking a question. Thus – CELL – PHONE?

And then there is, "Boy talk." Certain conversations are for males only. He does not like to talk about girlfriends, or trips to Hooters, or any number of "manly" topics in front of women. He is quite discreet that way. It's an old-fashioned, gentlemanly charm, an actual shyness. Or maybe he just doesn't want his girlfriends to know about all of his other girlfriends. Whatever the reason, "boy talk" is fun talk for Freddy.

Sometimes Freddy's gestures are as entertaining as his words. This is especially true if secrets are involved. He loves sharing secrets, and while most people have, at some time, made the motion of "zipping the lips," few can do it with the flare he brings to the "operation." His lips pout out, his eyes twinkle, and the zipper zips. Sometimes he locks them after he zips them, just for maximum security.

He is also a great shusher and a prolific pointer. In fact, no one points quite like he does, or as often.

Freddy points at people when they walk in the room. He points when he talks to them, especially if the word, "you" is involved. "You did it," or "You ball game," will often be accompanied by the Freddy point. Sometimes the point is one finger extended from a tightly clinched fist, a fist that, in time, becomes unclenched. The wrist then goes limp. At that time, the wrist bends, and all his fingers point downward, as if they are "at ease."

He likes the word "bull." Not Bulls, as in his term for Anderson County, but bull as in . . . well . . . not true, or something along those lines. For example, if someone says the Dragons are going to lose a game, his answer may be "Bull no." Sometimes, "Bull" is really, "Buuuullllll."

One of the funniest "Fredisms" occurs when he suddenly realizes something he had not realized previously. Sometimes he will literally call a time out, complete with the correct gesture. Other times he will say, "Hold on a minute," only it doesn't come out that way. The word "hold" sometimes loses the "l" sound, and the word "on" may disappear. So "hold on a" morphs into "hoduh." "Minute" sounds more like "mint." Thus, if things need to slow down, "Hoduh mint" usually does the trick.

When things have slowed down, and all is right again, Freddy may answer questions with the word "okay." That word has never sounded more genuinely happy than it does when he says it. Sometimes the "o" is optional. So a conversation with a friend (A.F.) might be:

A.F.: Do you want to go to Hooters now?
Freddy: Okay!
A.F.: We'll leave in two minutes.
Freddy: 'Kay!
A.F.: Maybe we should stay home instead.
Freddy: Buuulll NO!
A.F.: Should I bring my wife?
Freddy: No. Boy talk.
A.F.: Alright. Just us men.
Freddy: 'Kay!
A.F.: Should we call someone else?

That's when the CELL PHONE comes out, and the calls to his friends begin. One interesting aspect of this involves Freddy's distinction between friends and family. His brother John says, "He won't to go to Hooter's with me – or the family -- only with buddies."

For those who cannot make the journey, pictures of Freddy with the Hooters girls may be sent via cell phone. That might lead to more boy talk about the bronde girl at Cougars. Or he might zip his lips and say nothing, quietly waiting until he can go home and watch a rerun of the Three Doo Doos.

One word that Freddy has become skilled at using is the word, "Scrooge." For him, it is not just a Christmas word; in fact, it is more likely to be used in conjunction with his birthday. The modifying word or words he uses to denote which specific type of Scrooge a person is may vary, but those who don't "deliver" at Christmas or birthdays are apt to be identified as Scrooge.

"Me quit" is one of Freddy's oft used expressions. It is ironic that such a doggedly determined individual would ever use those words, but he does. He used them often when he was forced to go to Daniel

Arthur and he didn't want to go. He used them to describe his status as a funeral home helper after "they" shot him.

"Come on Freddy, time to go to school."
"Me quit."
"Freddy – are you still working at the funeral home?"
"Me quit."

Freddy likes to go to a restaurant famous for its steak and Australian cuisine. To most people, it is called Outback. To Freddy, it is Back Back.

Finally, there is another two-word phrase that is germane to an understanding of the uniquely rich vocabulary that is Freddy's. It is not a pretty phrase. In fact, it is, in some ways, the lowest common denominator for what passes as humor in countless movies and comedic performances. The truth is that Freddy loves body function, bathroom humor – especially during "boy talk." He loves it when people . . . or animals . . . well . . . fart. Break wind. Flatulate. Toot. Whatever euphemism is used, it does not compare with the way Freddy expresses it. To him, passing gas is the same as actually having a bowel movement. In both cases, Freddy will use two words. Those words are, "Shit one."

Want to make Freddy laugh? Fart. Want to make him giddy? Bring in camels for a nativity scene – camels that don't conform to societal norms – camels that pass gas and actually defecate whenever and wherever they choose. Freddy is a fan, and at each and every tacky step of the way, he will be there to point out that the beasts, "Shit one."

The fact that Freddy uses one phrase for two different bodily functions is not, in the overall scheme of life, a big deal. But it does make for some interesting "theatre." Ask Alvin Taylor. Late in the 2011 baseball season, Alvin was the chauffer du jour for the umpteenth time. They were heading home when a stop at Wendy's became "necessary." They entered. Freddy immediately went to the bathroom. By the time he was done, Alvin was on the other side of the restaurant. That did not stop Freddy from looking across the way before yelling, "Hey – Hey Coach. Me shit one."

Perhaps too much information was exchanged. Certainly, customers were treated to an unusual "late breaking bulletin of a personal nature." But Freddy was just being Freddy. He has a way with words – even tacky ones. Bull yeah.

The Great Communicator

He is the most quoted man in Clinton – perhaps all of Anderson County. And if imitation is the sincerest form of flattery, he is clearly the most flattered.

Experts, like Jody Wright, consciously imitate him. So do his friends and relatives. But an incredible number of people utter words or phrases that are truly Freddy-inspired without thinking about it. All that is required is to spend some time in his presence, and listen carefully, and before long, his speech patterns take over. And it can start at an early age.

For Luke Hatmaker, the imitation began at age three. Luke is the son of former Dragon athlete Brian Hatmaker and former C.H.S. cheerleader Mary (Hennessee) Hatmaker, so Freddy has known the parents since their high school days. It was only natural that he would stop and talk to them when they were picking up their son from nursery school.

The First Baptist Wee Ministry is across the street from Freddy's place. He often cuts through the parking lot during his daily adventures around town. This particular outing led him to the Hatmaker's van just as they were buckling Luke into his car seat. When it was time to leave, Freddy tapped the window by the car seat and offered his sincere, touching, parting words to Luke. The exact words were, "Bye Punk."

Freddy will use the word "punk" when he is mad, but he will also use it jokingly, as he did in this case. In most cases, it would have been an unremarkable event. In Luke's case, it became a phrase to repeat – and repeat – and repeat. He would walk around the house saying, "Bye punk." Then he would whack whatever was closest to him.

On Mother's Day, the Hatmakers went to visit Mary's parents, (and Luke's grandparents), Nancy and Joe Harper. Luke had been coached to wish Nancy a Happy Mother's Day. And he did – Freddy-style. He walked in, looked at Nancy, and said, "Happy Mother's Day – Punk." Then he slapped the wall.

"Punk" became the punctuation mark for other phrases and sentences – and the voice sounded very much like the originator of the tender term.

Some people have trouble saying the word "ready" without adding a little Freddy-flair. If someone asks, "Are you ready?" it is tempting to answer, "Me ready." The word "ready" begins with the "r" being rolled, or at least exaggerated, so that the first syllable of the word consists of a dominant "r" sound that lasts many seconds, followed by a quick "eady."

People will answer questions with, "Me no," or, "Shoot yeah," or "You out." Clinton High School students will use those phrases. Adults – parents and grandparents – will use Freddyisms. Sometimes they do so purposely, for effect, for the humor of it. Sometimes it just happens. It is never mean-spirited. People are always laughing with him, not at him. But one thing is clear. Freddy literally affects the way people in HIS town communicate, and that is as true for senior citizens as it is for three-year-olds. Perhaps Margaret Calhoun said it best: "Speaking 'Fredish' is a natural part of our family's communication. It has been passed down from father to son to grandson, all with a gentle humor and much love."

Apples and Roosters

Linda Long is the youngest of two sisters and two brothers. She is ten years younger than Freddie, but that didn't stop them from making memories during the dog days of summer. She is also Football Boy Jason Rhodey's aunt. She shares the following tale from a time when she was five or six years old:

"Our daddy, Carl Taylor, Sr. laid carpet at the time for Mullins Carpet in Clinton, and Freddy's daddy did also. Freddy would walk almost daily to play with us. We were very poor and struggling, like most people were. We were fortunate enough to have different trees and bushes in our yard – cherry, peach, apples, blackberries, muscadines (which Freddy hated) and wild strawberries. We also had quite a few pets, some of which were unusual. We had skunks for awhile, and we had a huge Rhode Island Red rooster. That rooster never let us play outside without attacking us.

"I remember one day the rooster had flogged me. The rooster was running toward Freddy and was in mid-flight, intent on landing on Freddy's back to flog him, and Freddy turned around and yelled, 'Stop.' The crazy rooster actually reversed flight somehow and ran from Freddy. It was funny."

Linda had a pet hamster that bit her finger. After it was bandaged Freddy kissed it three times.

They had chicks, and one metal pole that stuck out from the other wooden poles and fencing. That pole was maybe fifty feet from the apple tree in the backyard. At least a dozen people would try to

159

hit that pole with the apples that had fallen from the tree. Freddy was the first to hit it, using that slingshot throw of his. Linda describes it as, "A gunslinger pulling his weapon for a showdown."

Freddy couldn't climb the trees, but Linda and her brother Jody would, and they would throw apples or cherries down to Freddy.

Sometimes he would just walk down the curvy country road, losing himself in the natural setting. Linda's father would give him a ride home. She describes Freddy as, "A boy of few words (then), a huge caring heart, and a love of nature." Of course she was one of his girlfriends. "Freddy was my family on some of those blistering hot summer days that will remain in our hearts and our memories forever."

It is hard to picture Freddy ever being a boy of few words, but that's what he was to Linda. Of course that was long before he was a mayor, or an ambassador. Back then, he was just a boy, enjoying a simpler time, throwing apples and yelling at a rooster, and impressing another girlfriend.

THE FAIR!!

The Anderson County Fair bills itself as, "The Best Six Days of Summer." Freddy would concur. In fact, it is hard to overstate his love for the fair.

His mother was once asked, "Which does Freddy get more excited about – Christmas or the fair?" It was not an easy question to answer. Barbara gave it considerable thought before siding with Christmas, but she could not be certain. He is like a child at Christmas when it comes to the fair.

One of the salient and refreshing characteristics of the fair's biggest fan is his tendency to look forward. He perpetually has something that excites him – something that merits a countdown. The countdown to the fair begins after the pool is ready, after his numerous birthday parties, after the list of those who have been tardy with this presents has been presented. He will continue to harp on those who have not delivered the gifts, but he will also focus on the six weeks or so that separate his birthday and the fair. "Three more" means that only three weeks remain until Freddy is in Fair Heaven.

The fair itself is surprisingly big for a small town. Many of the attractions are typical of such events. The fair has livestock shows, a demolition derby, myriad rides, truck and tractor pulls, lawnmower races, and numerous musical acts. There is a Fairest of the Fair beauty contest for Freddy's girlfriends to enter. There are prizes for art, crops, flowers and photography. And there is food. Lots of food. And large crowds. In other words, it is everything a social animal like Freddy could ask for, and he cannot wait to be in the middle of all that activity.

In 2011, the fair celebrated its 123rd birthday, making it one of the six oldest fairs in Tennessee. For twenty years, Steve Queener has been associated with the Anderson County Fair; the last seven years he has been its president. That alone qualifies him to be an important element in Freddy's world, but there is far more to their relationship than that.

Steve is the Clerk and Master for Anderson County. He is also the supervisor of basketball officials for the Tennessee Secondary School Athletic Association (TSSAA). Consequently, he gets to see and talk with the officials who work basketball games with Freddy in attendance. He smiles with satisfaction at the way the experienced referees have learned to enjoy Freddy and his antics, and he chuckles when he recalls how the rookies have to learn to adjust to his presence. He may not be quite as vocal as he is at baseball games, but he is an effective heckler and critic.

Steve is a Clinton guy – a true Dragon fan. He is a C.H.S. graduate who played basketball for Coach Don Lockhart. He estimates that he has known Freddy for about forty years. He is also Jody Wright's brother-in-law, and he was a witness to the Coke spill and the subsequent flipping off when Jody honked at Freddy.

Steve recalls a time, back in the mid 80's, when he was the Director of Park and Recreation. He would often drive through the parks after dark, making sure everything was okay. He would often find Freddy – sometimes walking, sometimes sitting at a picnic table, relaxing. He recalls one night when he found Freddy after he had been beaten up. He rushed to his aid, and Freddy told him, "Boys hit me. They gone." All these years later, he still marvels at the inhumanity of someone who could do such a thing to a person like Freddy.

Fortunately, Freddy wasn't hurt badly. Fortunately, that incident would be one blip on an otherwise crystalline radar screen. Fortunately, there is the Anderson County Fair. The fair can make up for a multitude of problems.

Growing up on Eagle Bend, it was a short walk from Freddy's house to the fairgrounds. It is only one mile from his place at The Towers to the fairgrounds – a distance that, until his hip injury, was not much of a challenge for him. So Freddy has always lived close to the fair, except for a short "experiment" with residence in Oak Ridge.

Prior to his 1984 entrance to The Towers, Freddy had actually moved into a place in Oak Ridge. It would not work, and the fair was at least partially responsible. Freddy would live there about a month. His stay ended when he realized his beloved fair was in town. Freddy's place in Oak Ridge was ten to fifteen miles away. Even in his prime, that kind of distance was a challenge. But the fair was not to be missed, so he started walking, stuck out his thumb, and hitched a ride to Clinton. Who picked him up, and what they discussed along the way is a matter for conjecture now, but clearly he was able to communicate enough to get to where he needed to be. That would be the end of the Oak Ridge residency. As Freddy so eloquently phrased it, "Me quit."

Planning for the fair is a year-round undertaking. Freddy is content to leave the details to the committee members. But the week before things get started, Steve and any number of other workers will be on site, making sure things are ready for the workers who will come in to set up the rides and the booths and the midway. At some point, as if some cosmic radar has detected their presence, Freddy will find them, and certain traditions will begin to unfold, even before the fair is set up. For example, does each person responsible for putting on the fair get a new shirt advertising the current fair? Absolutely. Do they always order an extra one for Freddy? Of course. Does he always come to collect? No answer required.

Freddy's presence at the pre-fair planning stage once provided Steve with his favorite Freddy story.

This particular gem involves a locked gate – a seldom used locked gate. Access through that particular side entrance was rarely needed, but for reasons long since forgotten, one year the gate needed to be opened. Steve tried all of his keys. He couldn't open it. He felt confident that the fair manager, Oscar Pointer, would have the solution. Oscar carried a huge ring of keys. He had keys to everything in the area, except the gate. After trying a ring full of keys to no avail, it became apparent that the next step might involve cutting the chain that held the lock.

Of course, Clintonians know how this story ends. They know that, once again, cosmic radar, or fate, or divine intervention would dictate that Freddy miraculously appear. They know, because they have heard of his other "key" moments, what happens next. At the time, Steve didn't know about all of Freddy's keys. He was joking when he asked Freddy if he could open the gate, and he was shocked when Freddy produced a ring comparable to Oscar's. But all of that paled in comparison to what happened next. "He tried one key – ONE KEY – and the lock was open. He knew exactly which key it was." For Freddy, it was just another day at the office. For Steve, it was another mind-boggling encounter. "I still have no idea where he got that key or how he knew which one it was." Problem solved. The fair must go on.

Oscar would be involved in another Freddy moment. Several years ago, Freddy was convinced that he should run away with the workers who set up the fair – his version of running away to join the circus. Joe credits Oscar with talking him out of that "career choice." The people of Clinton remain grateful.

The fair always begins on a Monday. That means the final preparations and set up are always on a Sunday. Who arrives, like clockwork, to supervise the set up? Who else? Steve points out that the crew working on the midway is from Alabama, and he adds, "They all know Freddy by name."

There is another fine tradition related to the fair. In addition to the shirt, each committee member has a name tag to identify himself or herself. Typical of so many people who find so many ways to make Freddy feel included, he too gets a name tag. Only his does not contain his name. His tag simply says, "**BOSS**." It is a touching tribute – something he wears with pride.

And then, the fair begins. He sees so many people, some of whom he hasn't seen since the last fair. It's time for corn dogs and cotton candy and girlfriends galore. He doesn't do too many rides, though he drives a mean bumper car if they are available. Not all events occur annually. Some, for a variety of factors, appear less frequently. Wrestling is one of those periodic events, and when it is part of the fair, Freddy's version of Wrestlemania makes all other versions seem tame. Steve recalls the last time it was part of the fair: "Freddy was in the ring, wearing a mask, yelling and carrying on and being part of the show."

That is the essence of the fair and his love affair with it. He may be found in the wrestling ring, or the dunking booth, or "helping" a worker run a booth or game, yelling at people to play "his" game. In 2010, the Parrot Brothers, an exceptional Jimmy Buffett cover band, allowed Freddy to do his best Elvis impersonation on their stage. He reprised the act in 2011. He is young again, energized again, reveling in the sounds and sights and smells of this slice of Americana. It is, indeed, the Best Six Days of Summer.

Random Acts of Fredness

When Freddy hitch-hiked from Oak Ridge to Clinton so that he could go to the Anderson County Fair, it was a typical spontaneous, free-spirited act that, in many ways epitomizes the way Freddy lives his life. It was certainly not the only such act. The consequences of those acts are varied, unpredictable, and often humorous.

One such random act occurred when Freddy was about twelve. Not surprisingly, it began at a baseball field. This particular field is across the street from the Community Center. Freddy was no stranger to the center, and at some point during the game he wandered across the street to use the bathroom. What happened next was so bizarre – and involved such strange timing – that it still baffles his relatives.

The first strange element is that no one noticed Freddy going into the center. For a boy who knew, even at an early age, how to attract attention, that was remarkable.

What Freddy didn't know was that he had walked into the center at closing time. What the person in charge of securing the building didn't know was that someone was in the bathroom. When Freddy came out of the bathroom, he discovered he was locked in. This was long before cell phones, so he had no way to call for help.

It was not unusual for Freddy to wander off. He was within walking distance of his house and many of his favorite places. But as time wore on, his family became concerned. Freddy was missing, and he would remain missing until the next morning when the center re-opened.

Freddy's keen sense of loyalty led to another unique decision. When his brother John had two tickets to see a Tennessee Titans exhibition game, he asked Freddy if he would like to go with him. John's offer was turned down. The reason? The Dragons were playing that day. The N.F.L. is no match for Freddy's beloved team. He calls them "My boys." Case closed.

Freddy attended Daniel Arthur until he was eighteen. He then attended a place called Highland View. This was a place where people were trained to do simple work-related tasks. He was only there for one year, but he left his mark.

One evening, Freddy's mom got a call from the school. She was told that things were going well and, as a result, the school wanted to take the students on a picnic. Barbara was asked if she would pack a lunch – which she was happy to do. Freddy was happy to take the lunch from the refrigerator the following morning. What Barbara did not know was what else Freddy took. His dad was still at home then, and there was beer in the refrigerator, and Freddy was going to need a drink, so . . . Who showed up at a school picnic with a beer? The one and only.

It should be pointed out that Freddy was not breaking the law at that point in time. In 1971, the State of Tennessee lowered the legal drinking age to eighteen. It was raised to nineteen in 1979 and back to twenty-one in 1984, so Freddy broke no law, although he stomped all over a school rule. The administrator who called Barbara wasn't mad – he just wanted to let his mom know what happened. Freddy would remain beerless for the rest of the year.

Retired Clinton Middle School physical education teacher Doris Mayes knows Freddy, although no one in Clinton ever calls her Doris. Since she was a five-year-old bat girl for a team her daddy was coaching, she has been known as Doodles. It started when her father said, "Doodle bug, why don't you get that foul ball for me." From that day until now, she, like Freddy, has been a single-name persona.

167

Clinton Middle School sits close to one of the busiest streets in town. It also is very close to Freddy's place. Doodles recalls how Freddy looked forward to spring, when she would start taking her classes outside for physical education. He enjoyed it when they started playing kickball. Like so many other situations, Freddy's radar would go off and he would wander over to the school, and before long he was the permanent pitcher for all of the kickball games. He loved it, and the junior high school students instinctively knew that Freddy was to be part of the fun.

Doodles had a wooden chair. So did her colleague, Barry Voskamp. They would take the chairs outside so they would have a place to sit between the games. Freddy had no such chair – but not for long. Eventually, a matching chair was found. They wrote Coach Number One on Doodle's chair, Coach Number Two on Barry's, and Coach Number Three on Freddy's. The proud third coach would often refer to himself as, "Coach Free."

In the 1980's, Doodles was able to secure a high school basketball tournament that would be hosted by C.M.S. Freddy would be with her from set-up to clean-up. One night he asked how many games were going to be played. It is important to remember that, for Freddy, even a single game is often referred to as, "Ball game – ball game." When she told him that there would be four games that night, he just shook his head and uttered, "Ball game, ball game, ball game, ball game. Phew. Ball game, Ball game." Of course he stayed until the games were over, the buses had left, and the lights were turned off.

In 1982, George Thorogood and the Destroyers had a hit song called *Bad to the Bone*. Even though Freddy's musical taste is more country oriented, he loved that rock song – and still does. C.H.S. coach and physical education teacher Susan Zellner remembers him requesting the song at half time during basketball games. This was back in the days when basketball half time meant Freddy was the entertainment, primarily with his shooting demonstration. But as Susan points out,

"He always wanted that song played so he could dance and do his Ric Flair walk."

Freddy doesn't do the half time show anymore, and the song may have faded into obscurity in his mind had it not been for baseball. The Dragons play music between each half inning as the pitcher takes his warm-up tosses while his fielders field and throw behind him. Recently, a new tape was made, and suddenly the driving, pulsating refrain of, "Buh Buh Buh Buh Bad – Bad to the bone . . ." came over the P.A. system. If Freddy had his way, it would be the only song played between innings. Amazingly, this is one instance where he did not get his way.

In addition to Elvis and Johnny Cash (especially the song *Walk the Line,* or *Walk the Rine* as he says it), he likes Ray Orbison's *Pretty Woman.* It may be that "growl thing" Orbison does. He likes Gretchen Wilson's *Here for the Party.* He likes church songs. If he is not watching a sporting event, odds are good that his T.V. will be on the Country Music Channel. Freddy loves music.

Recently, while riding with Alvin Taylor, an old Sonny and Cher song came on the radio. Freddy's response? "Shame." That single word demonstrates a remarkable insight into Freddy's abilities. He heard a song that he had not heard recently. He made a connection to the singers, and then made the connection to the tragic event associated with one of them. It also shows how compassionate he truly is. Sonny Bono had been dead for over a decade (he died in 1998). Yet there was Freddy, remembering the artist and his death and succinctly describing the situation. He continues to amaze.

One person amazed by Freddy, and Freddy's ability to remember things is C.H.S. graduate E.T. Stamey. Mr. Stamey is an educator, a member of the Clinton City Council and Vice-President of the Anderson County Fair Association. He first met Freddy when his son, Tim, was playing middle school football. For reasons known only to Freddy, he decided that his "duty" for that season was to carry Tim's equipment. That was thirty years ago, but when Tim came back in town for a reunion, he saw Freddy, whose first words were, "Oh my God – you."

He then pantomimed the motions of carrying equipment, leaving E.T. to comment, "I am blown away by this memory."

E. T. is not alone. At some point, anyone who spends significant time with Freddy Fagan will, in fact, be "blown away." It might be because of his memory, or his kindness, or his humor. It might be because of the unbridled happiness he shows and shares at the myriad special moments in his life. It might be because, at some point, people feel a need to stop and consider the proverbial "big picture," to reflect on where Freddy has been, and where he is today; to see the growth and the acceptance – and the joy he brings to an entire community. It is in those moments that one is forced to reflect on his or her own growth and contribution. That's when the realization sets in. This is <u>not</u> just another love story. It is far bigger than that. It encompasses far too many people, touches far too many hearts. It takes an extraordinary teacher to teach those things. Freddy makes it look easy.

The Prankster – Part II

Dennis Pratt is at it again. This time it is another Presidential memo. Previous administrations have delivered a similar message, but this time it is Barack Obama's turn. The "official policy statement" reads:

Due to a waning economy, several dates must be omitted from your 2011 calendar in order that America can preserve precious oil, gas and electricity. All activities on those dates must be discontinued under the authority of federal law. Any infraction of this law will be penalized by fine and imprisonment. The dates to be omitted are as follows:

May 30, 2011
July 11, 12, 13, 14, 15 and 16, 2011

The Presidential order ends with a, "Thank you," followed by Barack Obama's "signature." There is a Presidential seal affixed to the document. It is the type of seal that barks and claps its flippers.

Freddy may not understand all of the words when they are read to him, but he will get the main idea. Once again, an American President has cancelled his birthday and all of the dates for the Anderson County Fair. Once again, Freddy will rail at the man he knows is behind this. "Punk Ryin' Jennon" strikes again. It also proves that distance is no obstacle when it comes to teasing his favorite target. In fact, "long-distance teasing" has a long-established precedent. It began more than two decades ago, when Dennis moved to Maynardville.

The Prankster admits that he quickly began to miss the daily encounters with Freddy, and that Freddy was missing his nemesis. There was a solution. As Dennis says, "Thank goodness for the fax machine."

Faxed insults became the modus operandi. There is glee in the telling of it: "One of the first interactions I started was when I drew a picture of Fred's head on the body of a fat ape. Boy, it was a good one, too. There was no mistaking who or what it was, and it got a great response."

The "great response" would be a photocopy of a human hand. The hand would be clenched, but the middle finger would be extended. Clearly, someone helped him find the "appropriate" response. Clearly, someone helped him address the fax, which read, "To Jennon." Clearly, Freddy signed it.

Freddy's writing ability extends to his name. It is written in a style that is as unique as the writer himself. It was used for the cover of this book. It was used in the title of *The Clinton Courier News* article – *My Name is Freddy*.

Freddy's ability to appear in his local newspaper is uncanny. Celebrities with expensive press agents don't get as much coverage as he does, and he is always proud of each appearance. Such was the case of the *My Name is Freddy* story, at least until Dennis got through with it. At the time, Dennis was still working in Clinton, so it was easy for him to "play" with the article.

The feature was displayed at Hammers. Freddy would proudly point to it each day. Then Dennis started playing with the name, or adding "features" to the picture. The coup de grace was changing the name to Freda, adding long hair, full lips, and a cigarette.

Events like this would lead to fights. Verbal fights. Physical fights. Freddy the Wrestler would go at Dennis the Prankster in no-holds-barred, all out, mortal combat. They would yell and cuss at each other. They would attack each other. They would work on fancy footwork and ways to pin each other. In the process, Dennis would learn great truths about his opponent.

The first thing he learned was that, "back in the day," Freddy had an incredibly strong right hand, and that if he let go with a haymaker, it was to be avoided at all cost. Failure to do so could be very painful.

He learned that Freddy fell down in slow motion. He would get off balance, struggle, unsuccessfully, to regain his balance, and fall in stages – with seconds passing before he fell into the next stage. This made catching him fairly easy.

He learned that, no matter how worked up Freddy got, he still had his chivalrous side when it came to women. This was demonstrated during a particularly heated battle. Just as the serious cussing began, Dennis recalls, "Suddenly, in the midst of this, Freddy began to flail his hands wildly, palms out in front of his chest, yelling, 'Shut it, shut it, shut it.' Then he looked at me and pulled his fingers across his lips as if to zip them shut. Then he nodded his head and looked behind me. When I turned around, there stood Margaret Calhoun, Don's wife. Freddy looked at her and grinned and simply said, 'Boy talk.'"

"Boy talk." Enough said. Case closed. To some, the exploits of Dennis Pratt may seem harsh, even cruel, but the truth is exactly the opposite. He knows the risk – that some may see him as a person who picks on someone who is "disabled." Dennis dismisses the word, and in his mind, so does Freddy. He says, "Freddy has a huge disdain for the stigma on himself and <u>knows</u> that he is much better than that. Freddy sees himself as 'One of the guys,' and anyone who spends any amount of time with him is completely obliged to accept him as just that."

Could it be that the Prankster has a soft side? That his teasing is the ultimate sign of affection? That Freddy loves it because he knows he is being treated like, "One of the guys?" Yes, yes, and yes. But that will not stop future Presidential memos from being written. Maybe Christmas and baseball season will be outlawed. Only the Prankster knows.

Birthdays and Swamp Rats

His full name is Winfred E. Shoopman, but like Freddy, no one uses his full name. Winfred inherited his father's nickname, and to all who know him, he is Wimp.

Wimp vividly remembers the first time he saw Freddy. It was 1975, and he was moving from Oliver Springs to Clinton. It was winter, and there was a young man walking down the street in shorts and a t-shirt, wearing no coat. He wondered if something was wrong, if the man needed help. He would learn that the man had all kinds of help, and that wearing a coat was just not his style.

Eventually, they would become friends. When Wimp coached a church league softball team, Freddy would come to watch. The team allowed him to hit. Wimp would explain the situation to the opponents, and if Freddy did hit the ball, they made sure that he got to first base – and beyond. It seemed that lots of fielding errors and errant throws occurred when Freddy participated. Perhaps this was training for the classic softball moment he had playing with Sleepy Williams' team.

The emotional side of Wimp surfaces when he talks about his saddest memory. It was the time in 1980 when Freddy's mom was in Vanderbilt Hospital and Freddy had to live with his uncle in Nashville. Wimp was sad to see him leave, and worried about how he would survive. Fortunately, Freddy would return. For Wimp, "It was a reunion – like a family member had come back . . ." He was not the only one who felt that way.

From 2001 – 2009, Wimp was Clinton's mayor, and he proudly takes credit for two monumental events in the life of Freddy Fagan. The two events are closely related, and they both brought considerable joy to the town. One continues to do so.

The first idea was to have a big celebration to honor Freddy's 50th birthday. It would be a party – held at Jaycee Park, and the town was invited. Hundreds came. It was covered by the local media, which is only fitting when a celebrity is being honored. The special catering talents of Vernon Long guaranteed great food was served. Wimp's favorite memory is the look in Freddy's eyes when he saw the huge cake that was made for him. Freddy pointed and asked, "Mine?" When he was assured that it was, indeed, his, his first impulse was to take it home. He had to be gently persuaded to allow the cake to be cut and shared with all of his well-wishers. He thought it was too pretty to cut.

Bob Williams was able to arrange for a special gift and presentation. He called on long-time friend and Tennessee football legend Dewey Warren. The "Swamp Rat" came through.

In his book *Legacy of the Swamp Rat,* author Chris Cawood describes Warren as, "Tennessee's first pure passing quarterback." He also gives an insight into his colorful nickname. Dewey's love of the water and outdoor activities in his Savannah, Georgia home caused an angered high school coach to say, "You're just like an old swamp rat." A statement like that in front of high school teammates = instant nickname.

The Swamp Rat would take over as Tennessee's quarterback at the end of the 1965 season. He would lead the Vols in '66 and '67. He would spend a year in the N.F.L. with the Cincinnati Bengals and move to the Continental Football League. When he returned to Knoxville, he became a popular figure on sports talk radio.

In other words, getting Dewey Warren to come to Freddy's party was a big deal. When Bob asked his friend to see if he could get some kind of present for the occasion, he wasn't sure what to expect – but he did not think it would be a brand new, official University of Tennessee football helmet – complete with the trademark power T. Bob would be with Freddy some time later when Coach Phillip Fulmer autographed it. It sits in a prominent location at Freddy's Place.

The other special event was the citation and the presentation of the street sign that would permanently honor Freddy. As mayor, Wimp had the opportunity to sign many special proclamations, but it is clear that this one was, and continues to be, special.

It was an unnamed street that Freddy walked daily. It did not require people to change addresses. It leads to one of Freddy's favorite places – The Apple Blossom Café. And if the location was appropriate, the name was perfect.

No one would have complained if the street sign read Freddy Fagan Road. It could have read street, or avenue, or boulevard. All of those would have been well received, but they were not selected. Instead, the word "way" was used. It is, officially, Freddy Fagan Way, and it should be. With all of the nuances in the meaning of that word, it is the perfect choice.

A party. A celebration. A street sign. Freddy Fagan Way. That is the Clinton way.

Mr. Facebook

During a discussion with colleague and author Ray Oliver, Lisa Harrison Smith casually mentioned the idea of creating a Facebook page for Freddy. In February of 2011, that idea became a reality. The resulting explosion of Facebook friends has been a tribute to the Freddy phenomenon.

Freddy had 500 new friends in a little more than a week. He had over 3,000 in the first six months. In an increasingly global society, where people are willing to travel and relocate, Freddy literally has friends all over the world.

He has friends in Texas and Florida, Connecticut and California, Oregon and Denmark. And all those friends tell all of their new friends about Clinton's favorite son, and his legend grows.

Freddy does not own a computer. He cannot read the messages people post, but he has seen his page. He knows the names of people who have written to him. He has seen the many pictures people have posted. He sums it up with a head-bobbing, chin stroking, huge smile and the word, "Gooood." He had over 500 birthday wishes. And if Ray or Lisa post something on his behalf, it is guaranteed to bring a host of responses.

His page has been carefully crafted to reflect his personality. Under the category "High School," it says, "Freddy Fagan High." Alvin Taylor University is the listed college, and under "Employers," it lists the Clinton Dragons, and under that heading there is a partial list of his responsibilities. They include: Number one fan, umpire, ref, and Grand Marshall. In the "About You" category, it says, "Me like girlfriends, girlfriends, sports, girlfriends. And Jane's." It is only a partial list, but he couldn't have said it better himself.

Freddy continues to add new Facebook friends. They continue to send him warm greetings, and even though he is not part of the high-tech, computer age per se, the high-tech world has embraced him. It is a wonderful way for Clinton natives to keep track of an important part of their world, no matter where they live. It is one more example of the loyalty he inspires – and the depth of concern people have for him. Freddy is a low tech man in a high tech world. Somehow, that seems appropriate.

The Photo Shoot

When Freddy was told that a book was being written about him, he responded with, "Gooood." He was told that books take a long time to write, and that he would have to be patient, and he was – for about one week. Then the questions started. "My book ready?"

He became like the kid in the car on a long trip asking, "Are we there yet?" He would tell people he was mad at author Ray Oliver. "Me mad. My book ready No."

One night, he and Sleepy Williams traveled to Oak Ridge to watch the Pussycats play in a basketball tournament. When the game was over, Ray would become one more Clintonian with a keepsake phone message. "Hey Ray. My book ready? Call me – cell phone, stop shattin' 'round." There is a pause, then, "Pussycats lost."

As the book got closer to being finished, the author called on his daughter's photography talents. The result would be a four hour photo shoot that almost defies description.

Katherine Oliver Birkbeck is an award-winning photographer. She has received numerous national and international awards for her work at weddings and her work with children. She is also one of Freddy's girlfriends – has been since the late 90's when she worked at Hammers.

The shoot was scheduled for the Monday after Easter. Freddy was excited on Good Friday. He was wired on Easter Sunday. When

John went to help Freddy get ready on Monday morning, he sent Ray a test message. "He is fired up."

The action began at Freddy's place. After a brief session there, John, Freddy, Ray, and Katherine walked to Hoskins. Freddy entered and he received the required royal treatment, complete with his favorite soft drink. He posed – he chatted – he charmed. He made sure that everyone knew his birthday was approaching. He even went so far as to point out items in the store that would be suitable presents.

When the Hoskins session was complete, the quartet headed back toward Freddy's place and Ray's truck. On the way, Freddy finished his drink. He now had an empty cup. As if by design, the group passed a garbage can with no lid on it. The can sat underneath a protective overhang. It was a target too inviting to pass by.

Freddy was about fifteen feet away when he stopped. He made an underhand motion, rocking his arm and the empty cup back and forth for several warm ups before his final wind up. He let go – hoping his cup would find the inviting can. Unfortunately, the cup was thrown too high. It headed toward the garbage can, but it landed on top of the protective overhang instead. That's when Freddy lost it. He initially covered his mouth with surprise, then uncovered it and let out an unbridled laugh of pure joy. The picture on the front cover of this book was snapped at that moment. It is indicative of Katherine's knack for capturing a moment, and Freddy's ability to create one.

Once everyone got over the hysterical reaction to the "missed basket," they piled into the truck and headed for the next stop – Alvin Taylor's home. When the traffic slowed their progress, Freddy lowered the window and made honking noises. When, coincidentally, the traffic moved again, Freddy reacted as if he had caused it. More fits of laughter. The window was raised and would remain raised for two or three more minutes, until Alvin's house came into view. Alvin was in the front yard, so it was imperative that the window be lowered and greetings shouted before the truck came to a stop.

There would be photos at the Taylors, and then across the street to the front of the house where Freddy used to live, then a quick ride to the baseball field. At every stop, his joy – his enthusiasm – his absolute happiness permeated every facet of the activity.

From the baseball field the group journeyed to Hammers. What might have been a quick session turned into a marathon, as Freddy spoke to countless customers, pointed to countless potential presents, and entertained Don, Don's girl, Bye Ran, Cruddy, and anyone else who happened to pass by.

When Freddy was *finally* extricated from Hammers, it was time to join Bob and Sleepy Williams at Jane's for lunch. Then it was off to visit his personal stylist, Marcus Mitchell, then a shot of his street sign, and then a trip to the football field. From there he would go back to the baseball field for pictures with the team. That would be the end of the line for the photography session, but Freddy would travel with the baseball team to an away game. It was just another day in the life of a celebrity, another opportunity to be a star, one more chance to make something as simple as taking a picture an adventure, an event, a happening.

Katherine's take on the Fredventure is quintessentially artistic. She says:

I guess you could call me someone who loves photography with personality. I knew when the idea of the photo shoot got tossed around that Freddy would give me personality. Sometimes adults are hard to photograph. They are awkward and just so aware of the camera that it is hard to capture their true emotions. This was not the case with Freddy. He would kick a football like there were hundreds of people in the stands. Or he would blush talking to the pretty ladies at Hoskins.

What I think makes Freddy so special to photograph is the fact that his personality is the brightest when he is with the people he has come to know, trust, and love. Watching Freddy joke with AlvinTaylor through a camera lens – priceless. Going to Hammers and watching him tell Margaret, Don and Kelly everything he wants for his birthday – now that is just an historic moment. I feel privileged to have captured what will be known as pieces of history in the town of Clinton.

And, well, I am Freddy's girlfriend, so of course I can make him smile.

The Tennis Match – Part II

Since Don Calhoun and Alvin Taylor have yet to be hired for a real radio or T.V. show, their hypothetical one continues. As it did for the first "show," this one takes the form of a tennis match.

This time, Alvin serves first. He reaches back more than three decades to deliver a story that goes back to his days of running the Jaycee Pool.

It was common for local groups to rent the pool "after hours," i.e. – for a specified period of time after the pool was closed to the general public. Numerous clubs and organizations would do so. Often, food would be involved – which meant that, often, Freddy was involved. He had been at the pool until closing, and he often just stayed on and made a "guest appearance" at the private party. He was almost always welcome. Alvin's story involves one time when he wasn't.

A local church group had booked the pool, and for reasons known only to them, decided that they did not want Freddy to be part of the festivities. Somehow, Alvin was given the unenviable task of informing Freddy of that fact.

This would create a red faced, vein-popping, lip quivering reaction. A livid Freddy began to cuss the church people. F-bombs were dropped. Freddy stormed out into the middle of Knave Street and sat down. He yelled and cussed and extended the middle finger. It is not one of Alvin's fondest memories, although it is one of the most vivid. Freddy cussing a church group. Freddy not being welcomed by them. Things have certainly changed.

It would be Don's turn to return the serve. He would start with a simple question: "Remember when Freddy and Foozie caught those fish?" For people who know the story, the answer is accompanied with a guttural reaction that is part laugh and part groan. For those who do not know the story, it is a classic. A very gross classic, but a classic nonetheless.

A successful fishing trip ended with fish that the two fishermen shared. Freddy took his share home to, presumably, be cooked and eaten. Theoretically, Freddy could get help with the preparation if he needed it. Only Freddy didn't get help. He may have lost interest, forgot, got lazy, or changed his mind. No one knows exactly what went through his mind, but the unprepared fish were unceremoniously dismissed to the confines of the garbage can. They would remain in the un-emptied garbage can until . . . well . . . until the cops came.

The fish did what uncooked fish do; they omitted a stench that would, in time, cause residents of The Towers to go from curious to grossed-out to fearful. The fear was that someone had died – maybe even Freddy. The police were called, surrounding apartments were checked, and finally the source of the ever-increasing fetid smell was discovered and disposed. Freddy was, remarkably, unfazed. Over the years, the incident has gone from gross to humorous. But for those at The Towers, it was not the least bit funny at the time.

After a commercial break (Bass boats or seafood restaurants?) Alvin would be ready for another serve. He would once again call on his days at Jaycee Pool.

This time, the incident would illustrate the single-minded focus that sometimes characterizes Freddy. The Jaycee Pool usually opens for the Memorial Day weekend. For weeks leading up to the grand opening, he will say, "Pool ready." "Pool ready" may mean the pool is going to be ready eventually, that it is close to being ready, or that it is actually ready. It just depends, but since pool readiness and Memorial

Day coincide with THE BIRTHDAY, excitement reaches a feverish pitch. Freddy will get so focused that he will mention the pool and his birthday countless times daily.

One year, back in the 70's, Freddy decided that he should be the first person to go in the pool. And that was that. "Me first," holding up one finger, and any and all methods of communicating his mantra became the order of the day – or the order of many days. Freddy had decided that he would be first, and he would, indeed, be first.

Because he is a masterful storyteller, Alvin will point out that the water used to fill the pool is frigid – that it takes days of warm weather to heat it. In other words, Freddy had been warned. Not that it mattered. Nothing was going to stop him, and nothing did. On the day of the grand opening, he was, indeed, the first person to jump in the recently filled pool. He took a running start, let out a war hoop, and jumped in the shallow end, only to surface quickly, yelling, "God damn cold!" He had succeeded in his mission. At least Steve Pyatt did not have to rescue him.

The comical image of Freddy exiting the pool never gets old. Don would show his appreciation for a story well-served -- then add one of his own. This one would go back to the days when video stores and movie rentals were just beginning.

Tri-County Cinema in Oliver Springs was a theatre and a rental store. It was one of the first in the area to sell giant satellite dishes.

On the day of Don and Freddy's Excellent Adventure, the two had travelled to Oliver Springs so that Don could rent a movie. As Don perused the offerings, Freddy became enamored by the satellite dish and the television programming. As he stood watching, a salesman approached, and immediately tried to sell Freddy a satellite dish. An amused Don got to watch as the salesman tried to convince the person who never wants to spend his own money to purchase the expense equipment.

For his part, Freddy politely nodded, or stroked his chin, or mumbled, "Mmm." The salesman just kept going – oblivious to the absurdity of the situation. He would say, "Suppose I told you that you could get over one hundred channels." Freddy would nod and stroke his chin. He is a world-class chin stroker. The salesman would give his best spiel about how easy it was to finance the satellite. More head nodding and chin stroking. The salesman said, "I can see you are a man who likes to watch T.V." Freddy stroked his chin. Finally, sensing a big sale, the man asked, "What would you say if I told you that you could have this at your house in three days?"

Freddy broke his silence. He deflated the salesman as only he can do. He answered the question with a succinct, "God damn yeah." It was only then that the salesman realized he would not be making a sale to this particular customer. After another commercial, (Netflix or DirecTV) it would be time for the guest of the week. This time it would be 1999 C.H.S. graduate Travis Murray. Travis works in Shelbyville as a substance abuse counselor. He fondly recalls, "I met Freddy about eighteen years ago while playing Little League baseball. He was always cutting up and having a good time. He was the same every time I saw him." Travis is not the first to mention the wonderful consistency that characterizes Freddy's nature. Then he adds an insight that is as touching as it is profound. He says, "My father never saw me play baseball, but my hero Freddy never missed a game."

After those insightful words, it would be time for The Man himself to update the audience about this latest exploits. He would tell them that in a span of about two weeks, the baseball team honored him at their banquet with a birthday cake, that the Jaycee Pool was ready, and that he had numerous birthday parties, including one at Jane's and one at Hooter's, that he and Alvin travelled to more games together than most people see in years, and that as soon as his birthday is over it is time to get excited about the Anderson County Fair.

The only missing ingredient from the show would be the girlfriend of the week. This week's winner would be Pam Miller, but calling her the girlfriend of the week would be like calling The Beatles a one-hit wonder. She is a long-time girlfriend, one who deserves her own chapter.

Pam

Pam Miller is not related to Chuck and Katherine Miller, but for years she worked at their restaurant. She was, and is, one of his girlfriends, only in her case, that relationship transcends the typical Freddy flirtation. In fact, the two share a colorful history, complete with adventures and secrets and parties. There is a depth to their relationship that is difficult to describe, although the fact that he calls her every night may be a good indicator of how special it is.

Pam was there in "the early days," when Freddy wasn't as popular as he is now. She has seen customers who were not happy when he was around. She recalls one lady who wouldn't sit with her husband if Freddy joined their table. That particular woman made some negative comments about him to Pam. That particular woman received a crash course in the world according to Pam Miller – a world that recognizes and celebrates the uniqueness that is Freddy.

Pam is not shy. She is not afraid to candidly address her past – a past that saw her as a wild party girl. She worked at a place that Freddy frequented – and he enjoyed her friendly personality, her humor, and her willingness to include him in her activities, including her parties.

Pam is brutally honest about those days. She admits to being an alcoholic. She says that several times a week, during her breaks, she and Freddy would go to a liquor store where she would buy booze. It would be their secret – they would zip their lips – and he would never tell on her.

Pam did not encourage Freddy to drink with her, but that does not mean that he didn't. Fortunately, things did not get out of hand with him. Unfortunately, they did get out of hand with her.

Pam no longer drinks – she has been sober since 1997. That was the year she became a born-again Christian – and that is the event she credits with saving her life.

1997 was also the year of the Ray Charles concert. Pam and a number of friends went to see the master entertainer. Freddy was one of them. They all worried about Freddy's frequent trips to the bathroom, and how it might interrupt the concert experience. They addressed the issue with him. This was before Pam had given up drinking, and she and her friends had some pre-concert libations. Not Freddy. She laughs as she recalls, "That night, Freddy was the only one who did not have to go to the bathroom during the show. Everyone else did." Freddy took great pride in that fact, and did not hesitate to point it out to the group.

When Pam told Freddy about her quest to find sobriety and salvation, he told her, "Me prayin'." When she told him she had found it, he said, "God did it."

Pam now works at Little China, one of the restaurants that relocated to a different part of Clinton, but little else has changed. He doesn't frequent her workplace as often, and she isn't the party girl anymore, but their bond is as strong as ever. That bond gets tested when she works extra hours and is not able to take one of his nightly calls. During a stretch of late shifts, an exasperated Freddy called his girlfriend only to once again reach the answering machine. Typically ignoring any perfunctory remarks, he launched into his message: "Gone, gone, gone . . . you always gone, gone, gone. Call me."

Chronologically, Pam and Freddy are close in age. They are close in other ways as well. Pam was there to see how Chuck and Katherine Miller took care of him. It is almost as if she learned from them and developed her own way to carry that forward. One thing is certain – in Freddy's eyes, Pam is no ordinary girlfriend.

More Road Trips

The world truly is Freddy's chauffeur – at least that part of the world where he reigns. It might be Bob and Sleepy Williams taking him on a classic trip to Wrigley Field, or Don Calhoun winding along a bumpy road with a tea-filled passenger, or Alvin Taylor taking him to yet another "Ball game, ball game," but Freddy has more "frequent driver miles" than most people on the planet. Any number of Clinton families have taken him to any number of events, and those events are not limited to local events.

For pomp, majesty, and crowd size, it is hard to beat the spectacle that is University of Tennessee football. Freddy has been one of the 100,000 plus at Neyland Stadium, and part of the 25,000 attending a U.T. basketball game. He has been to U.T. baseball games, and Lady Vol games. The Chicago Cubs AA baseball team that plays in Sevierville? Been there, and done that many times. The Knoxville Ice Bears of the Southern Professional Hockey League? Of course, and there are shirts to prove it.

Thanks to Ron Mitchell, Freddy can claim two other road trips. One was a rather uneventful trip to Nashville to see the National Hockey League Predators play. The other trip was an eventful trip to Atlanta to see the Braves, a trip that would provide another classic moment.

Ron is friends with a Knoxville A.M. radio sports talk host named Tony Basilio. In fact, it was on the Basilio show when Freddy answered a question about the upcoming Clinton vs. Oak Ridge football game with the immortal words, "Damn Pussycats." When Tony decided to arrange a bus trip to an Atlanta Braves game, Ron knew that he would go, and that there was no doubt who he would take with him.

Ron has known Freddy for years. He is also good friends with Pam Miller. He has many fond memories of Chuck Miller and the times he and Chuck used to tease Freddy. Dennis Pratt is not the only one to tell him that his favorite events were cancelled. Once, Freddy was on the phone and Ron told him that Christmas was cancelled. Freddy's responded with, "Bullshit, Ron." Ron would later learn that Freddy made his eloquent response on the steps of the church he was about to enter.

One year, as the fair was about to begin, Chuck and Ron told him the fair was cancelled. They may have overdone it, because ultimately, Freddy got mad enough to throw a chair and storm out. They expected him to come right back. When he didn't, Ron went to look for him. He was at the fair site, as if to prove to himself that it was still coming. Apologies were made and accepted and the friendship was renewed.

Their friendship really developed in 1996. That was the year Ron had to stay out of work for an extended period of time – the result of a serious foot injury caused by a forklift. While he was recuperating and rehabilitating, he would spend increasing amounts of time with Freddy. By the time the opportunity to see the Braves arrived, they were good buddies.

The travelers got on the bus in Knoxville. Did a significant number of people instantly recognize Freddy? Of course. Would the rest know him by the time the journey was complete? Absolutely. But for Ron Mitchell, this trip will be forever etched in his memory because of one four letter word.

It was early in the post 9/11 world. It was the beginning of what is now the all too familiar screening and searching process that accompanies sporting events. Freddy had a camcorder with him. It was in a large bag. There was some debate about whether he would be allowed to enter with such a device. They decided to try. They waited in line as the security guards looked through purses and used their wands to check people. Ron said, "Freddy, let me take the bag. And let me do the talking." Freddy agreed, all the while observing what was going on around him. They got to the front of the line. Ron opened the bag. The guard was starting his search. That's when Freddy blurted out, "Hey pal – no bomb in there."

Bomb was the four letter word that – then and now – was NOT to be taken lightly. It has been known to cause major complications – including visits to the F.B.I. As a rule, security guards do not see any humor in that word – for obvious reasons.

Ron got the adrenalin rush that comes from such anxiety-producing situations. He immediately started explaining. Fortunately, the guard was an observant and understanding one. In fact, he actually did see some humor in it, and waved them through. Ron was so relieved he hugged the guy. There is no doubt that some guards might have made a bigger issue out of it.

When they were safely inside, Ron stopped and asked Freddy, "What were you doing?"

Freddy had the perfect answer: "My booboo."

There was nothing he, nor anyone else could do, except laugh. It is a typically funny moment. Freddy did what he so often does – he disarms people – even security guards. What is especially interesting is his language. It was not typical of his speech. The, "Hey pal" is unique, and the clear, concise, "No bomb in there," is a departure from the more traditional, "Me bomb no," or some variation there of.

That incident was not the end of the story. Once he got beyond the bomb, the second thing that Ron recalls is the heat. The temperature on the field was 100 degrees.

The third memorable aspect of the road trip was the best aspect for Freddy. That's because one of his absolute, all-time favorite baseball players was pitching that day for the Braves.

Freddy has excellent taste in baseball players. He loved Johnny

Bench and Greg Maddux during their playing days. He loves Chipper Jones, and "Bud's boy" Todd Helton. But he was absolutely crazy about John Smoltz, and he was on the mound that day. The fact that Freddy and his favorite pitcher both wore beards is probably just coincidence. When the game ended, Freddy did not talk about the victorious Braves. Instead, he informed people, "My boy won."

When the game ended, the group adjourned to the E.S.P.N. Zone for dinner. When the meal was over, Ron discovered that a member of the group had paid for everyone who was eating at Freddy's table. Ron can not recall the gentleman's name, only that he said he had enjoyed the trip and Freddy's company so much that he just wanted to treat them.

It was another day at the office for Freddy. He entertained his fellow travelers, skirted trouble with a security guard, watched his favorite pitcher, and ate for free. Not a bad day's work.

Freddy would make one more deposit in Ron's memory bank that day.

After a long bus ride down, hours in the hot Atlanta sun, a big meal, and a long bus ride home, Ron did what many others did – he fell asleep. When he awoke, he was greeted by his pal, who promptly told him that he snored like a pig. It's those tender moments that mean so much.

There would be other road trips. For a while, Ron had a boat, and just as Foozie Stair had done, Ron allowed Freddy to be the captain. When he thought Ron wasn't looking, he'd tap the throttle forward just a little, trying to go faster. Ron admits that he would find ways to make Freddy stand up or turn quickly so that his hat would blow off. Freddy's typical response was, "Damn you, pal," just as the boat was turned to retrieve the windblown and now wet hat.

Anyone who spends time with Freddy has his or her own version of Fredcabulary. Everyone hears words and phrases differently. Ron has his favorite. To him, Freddy's attempt at the word, "ambulance" comes out as, "cattle ranch.'" Freddy has had his share of cattle ranch rides.

Ron's final road trip memory may not have the dramatic effect of,

"Hey pal – no bomb in there," but it does have its moment. Ron and his wife and another family decided to take Freddy on a short journey to Anderson County Park, where they would camp overnight. Things were fine until the next morning, when Ron awoke to find that Freddy was not in the tent. Mr. Independence was doing what he always does – he was keeping pace to his own drummer.

Ron made a hasty search of the campgrounds and discovered him sitting at the table of other campers – eating breakfast. He would learn that this was not the first campsite he had blessed with his presence. The Mitchell contingent had "slept in." Freddy had not. Just like at Jane's, or Hoskins, or the E.S.P.N. Zone in Atlanta, Freddy was enjoying another free meal. Some of the other campers knew him. Others? Well . . . Freddy doesn't meet many strangers.

It is a variation on the theme – the second or third verse to a never-ending song. Freddy travels. He travels because people enjoy his company. His life is often richer than the lives of those who do not have his challenges. Wherever he goes, he sees people he knows. Wherever he goes, he meets new friends. And in the process, those who felt a desire to do something for Freddy realize that, in the end, he has done far more for them. Knoxville. Nashville. Chicago. Atlanta. Anderson County Park. Downtown Clinton. It does not matter. The setting may change, but Freddy never does. In a world of spin doctors and image makers and style over substance, Freddy is a refreshing alternative. No wonder he is so popular.

Random Observations

How does a person capture the essence of Freddy Fagan? It may be, as Jimmy Buffett so eloquently says in his song *Manana,* "Like trying to describe the ocean if you've never seen it." Many have tried; in fact, it is almost a community pastime. Here are some of the MANY comments people have made about Clinton's favorite son:

> *"The reality of Fred is that Fred has nearly no 'poker face' about him. If it's on Fred's mind, then it's on Fred's face."*
>
> Dennis Pratt

> *"To Freddy,*
> *A great Vol*
> *1998 National Champs"*
>
> Phillip Fulmer on Freddy's U.T. helmet

> *"He is one of our people – a fixture in our store and in the town of Clinton."*
>
> Helen Hammer

> *"If you have a problem with Freddy's hair, call me. Freddy chooses his own hair styles."*
>
> Handwritten note by Marcus Mitchell on the back
> of his business card, written to Freddy's family

"*Every year, Dave and I go to Daytona for The Daytona 500 speed week. The first thing that Dave does is buy Freddy a shirt.*"

Steve Queener

"*I remember Freddy waiting for us after school during the basketball season to go to Dairy Queen before the games. If Casey Taylor was going, Freddy was going.*"

Kristi Clark

"*It's funny how the tales of a good soul like Freddy can make you feel at home again.*"

Kymber McMurray

"*I have spent many hours sitting at sporting events in Clinton, especially baseball with Freddy . . . If you ever take the time to know him, he will always remember you and be a loyal friend.*"

Lisa Powell

"*Freddy would not be the person he is today without the great people of Clinton who have loved, supported, and cared for him, and for that our family is very grateful.*"

(Sister) Angela Poole

"*My family owned King's Pizza on Main Street, beside Hoskins, years ago. My grandfather, George Blankenship, was a softball coach for the King's Pizza Team. . . Freddy would be at every game, then we would always have pizza after the games. Even as a child I knew he was a special man.*"

Alena Kotopoulos

"*Freddy used to be afraid of the mannequins in the window of my shop on Main Street (My Sister's Closet). He would make loud noises and obscene gestures at them as he passed by at least once a day. . . Lately, I guess he has gotten to know us better and waves hello to "the girls" as he passes by."*

Catherine Parker

"Growing up next door to Freddy, I have been his, 'girlfriend' since I can remember. What a shame to know I'm not the only one. Coming home to visit a few years ago, I immediately ran into Freddy at a ball game. He recognized me and called me his girlfriend. I knew I was home."

Nicole "Rhyne" Frederik

"I'll never forget Freddy coming to a revival I was preaching in. He went into the choir and sang, then joined me at the altar to give the invitation. A memory I'll never forget and I'll cherish forever."

Beulah United Methodist
Preacher Steve Evans

"When the Dallas Mavs won the N.B.A. title, I bought a Dallas Mav t-shirt for Freddy. I gave it to him and he said, 'tomorrow. . .' which I knew meant he'd be sporting the shirt the next day. Freddy and his sport shirts!!! Ten years ago, when I told him I was moving to Dallas, he pointed to his chest and said, 'Cowboys.' I knew what he meant. . . My first trip back to Clinton, I saw Freddy on the street. He had not forgotten about the Cowboys. He pointed to his chest again and I whipped out his Cowboy's sweatshirt, which he wore while leading the parade the next day. Freddy never forgets a promise. His memory is amazing. I am so proud to be from Clinton. Any town that loves and protects its own, like Freddy, is the best!"

Donna Hall Leon

"Freddy fancied himself assistant band director beginning in the Stanley Barnes days. So, as the band crossed the field to begin pregame or halftime, Freddy always came with us. One night the band was in the middle of the show. It was during the ballad, the most

quiet and pretty section of the music. Freddy noticed someone had walked onto the field. So, in true band director fashion, he yelled at the top of his voice, while pointing to the band, 'Hey boy – damn band!' I can't remember the rest of the show that night."

Former band director, Tim Paul

"Hey Freddy – take off your sweater."

(Brother) John Fagan (with help from certain in-
laws) commenting on Freddy's hairy body

"Freddy will love you whether you give him a present or not. He is a real person – not to be pitied. He admires those who treat him like anyone else."

Don Calhoun

"Clinton is different. Freddy is different. And in a world that often doesn't willingly embrace being different, our small town defies such odds, and we can thank Freddy for teaching us that lesson."

Lisa Harrison Smith

"He can tell if you are laughing at him or laughing with him."

Jody Wright

". . . When I would see Freddy out walking late at night I made a point to pick him up and take him home. Since Freddy knew me, I believe he felt safe and would always accept a ride. At that time, I was not very keen on keeping a clean vehicle. The backseat was littered with all sorts of fast food bags, empty drink bottles and such. One night, Freddy got in, looked at the backseat, saw the mess, and said, 'Oooh – car a damn wreck.' "

Steve Corker

"I had the pleasure of meeting Freddy at my parents' shoe shop on Market Street in the early 90's. I was around fourteen, and Freddy

197

was always downtown. He would come in and get shoes from my dad. At some point he started saying I was his girlfriend. He always had a big hug to share when he came into the store. He would play H-O-R-S-E with us at the Clinton Community Center. Clinton would not be the same without him."

Amanda Barnett West

"One of the main reasons I was excited about moving to Clinton was because of the way the town treats Freddy."

Jim Harris

It is impossible to calculate the number of lives Freddy has touched. Even those who don't have a specific story have memories or feelings about his presence – his warmth – his humor. That is his gift to the town that loves him.

Cat

Freddy is always busy. He coaches. He directs the band. He is the town's social chairman. He has a plethora of girlfriends to entertain. He has calls to make and people to visit. And now, he has a cat to care for.

When Chuck and Donna began the process of moving from Chattanooga to Norris, they discussed what to do with Scalla – their black cat. Trying to move into one house while selling another created logistical problems for "kitty care." Freddy heard the discussion and let it be known that he wanted the cat. And so it came to pass, in the late spring of 2011, that Freddy would become a Cat Person.

Of course, Freddy owning a cat created more work for his family members, especially John. Freddy's not real keen on emptying the litter box or grooming the cat, but a little extra work for the family is a small price to pay for the opportunity to see the interaction between Freddy and his new feline friend.

One of his first duties as a cat owner was to change the name to something he could pronounce. In his typically succinct manner he dubbed his pet, "Cat." Sometimes it's, "Black Cat," or "Girl Cat," but usually plain old Cat will suffice.

There is another important duty Freddy faithfully performs. He has become a news correspondent of sorts. It all began when Joe moved to Florida.

Joe still gets his hometown newspaper. It is delivered by mail, but he notes that, by the time the paper has arrived, Freddy has often given him "the scoop" on some of the latest news during his daily "briefings."

For example, when Brad Kidwell (the groom Freddy slapped high five as he walked down the aisle at this wedding) became a policeman, Freddy covered the story. He reported, "Two-two cop." Joe would read the details later, but Freddy broke the story.

Perhaps that explains, at least in part, why Freddy is such a uniquely popular figure. He really does care about his town and what goes on. He cares about the people. He wants to be in the action – and he usually is. His status as the most quoted and imitated figure in Clinton has been established. But the nuances and subtleties never cease – and they never cease to amaze.

A person is fired. A group of people are talking about it. It is not uncommon for someone in the group to refer to the firing by imitating Freddy's, "You out!"

"Me no" is a common answer for those who associate with Freddy, and Freddy does not have to be in attendance for people to use it. "Are you going to the fair tonight?"

"Me no."

When Freddy wants to hold up three fingers, he consistently makes a circle with his thumb and first finger and holds up the last three (i.e. – the middle, ring, and pinkie). His brother Joe does the same thing. Initially, it may have been an unconscious action, but now that he is aware of it, he does it on purpose, just because Freddy does.

Joe is also aware of another endearing Frediosyncracy. It involves his love of ice cream – or ching-chong. He points out that the odds are always good that he has ice cream in his freezer. The odds are also good that he has scooped some into a large drinking glass, stuck a spoon in it, and put it back in the freezer. That way when the ching-chong craving starts, he can reach in, grab it, and start eating.

It is another look at yet another facet of Freddy's life. This is the more domestic version – the one where Freddy is sitting at home, eating his ice cream and talking to brother Joe in Florida while watching the Braves and/or listening to country music. And all the while, Cat is pacing, or sleeping, or purring, or hiding.

Freddy and Cat. It's a match made in Clinton.

Memory

For any family, trying to select the defining images of a family member is difficult. Memory is not an exact science. Images may become distorted over time. Special moments may be forgotten. Yet even if specific events are forgotten, impressions remain. The lasting impression left on each member of the Fagan family is that their life stories are richer because Freddy was written into them. Maybe one of Joe's fondest recollections epitomize the family's fondness for Freddy. It's a memory of a young boy at church. Joe reports, "He sang. He just always sang. He might not know any of the words, but he sang anyway." He adds, "He still does that."

The family remembers the time Freddy called Joe to tell him, "Me rich." Freddy often has money, so, "Me rich" is a common refrain, but this time, Joe was convinced that Freddy had a check. Then Freddy started to count the zeroes – one, two, three . . . Joe became interested. Four, five, six . . . The short-lived vision of Freddy the millionaire ended when Joe discovered the cause of the excitement. Freddy did, indeed, have a check. It was the non-redeemable, strictly for promotional purposes check issued by Publishers Clearing House. So close.

A family is often greater than the sum of the individual parts, and family stability may arise from unstable situations. The Fagan siblings were born in Germany, France, New Mexico, and Tennessee, but even when the family was finally stateside, they were not done moving. In 1961, they lived in Norris. In 1962, they moved to Eagle

Bend Drive in Clinton. In 1968, they moved to Chattanooga. In 1969 they moved back to Eagle Bend. Then they were settled.

One of the things the Fagan siblings learned was that escaping trouble at home could be as easy as blaming Freddy. Freddy might not get punished for certain things that other children would. So Joe, Angela, and Donna learned to say, "Freddy did it" when it suited their purpose. Freddy would have to wait until John was little, but eventually he was able to return the favor by saying, "John did it." Only John would go through life without a scapegoat.

The defining images from the past may be best expressed by the present for his two sisters. Angela has spent her entire career in education, but during the 2011-2012 school year, Donna re-joined the profession after a long absence. For the first time, both sisters are working together at the same school. Both of them are educators today because of the influence and the inspiration of growing up with their oldest brother.

John also has a defining image. As a junior high school student he wrote a paper about the most inspiring person he knew. Freddy was that person.

He unifies. He inspires. How? By being himself. By being uninhibited. By singing – even when he doesn't know the words.

Barneys, Barneys, Barneys

It is not surprising that many of the people who know Freddy well are police officers. Freddy has, for decades, roamed the streets of Clinton. He has done so at all hours of the day and night, and invariably, he would meet the police. They also have a presence at the events he loves the most – athletic events, the fair, and any place where crowds need to be managed.

Anderson County and the City of Clinton both have their own police force – not that it matters to Freddy. He treats both of them the same, and both of them look out for him. Both forces are quite capable of teasing him, just as he is quite comfortable calling them, "Cops" or, "One Bullet Barneys."

His previously mentioned fascination with the trappings of law enforcement – the gun, badge, cuffs, and whistle clearly make him happy. It also entertains those who enforce the law.

Mark Lucas is the Chief Deputy for the Anderson County's Sherriff's Office. He offers the following insight:

"It wasn't long ago when one of our 'new' deputies came into my office after having lunch at the Apple Blossom. He asked, with a curious look on his face, 'Did you know Freddy is wearing one of our badges?' 'Yes,' I replied. He continued to stand there with a puzzled look. So I finished, 'Who do you think gave it to him?' He turned and walked out without saying a word. I waited until he left before laughing out loud. Of course, he didn't know that I gave Freddy my badge years ago,

I guess it was sometime in the mid 80's, along with one of my pairs of handcuffs that he has."

Just like Clinton City Chief Scarbrough cares deeply about Freddy, so does Anderson County Chief Deputy Lucas. He adds, "I am very proud to call Freddy my friend."

Eddy Stair has another look at Clinton's icon. He says:

"I was a Reserve Police Officer for the Clinton Police Department for twenty-two years, from 1974 to 1996. One night in mid-summer in the early 1980's, I was riding the midnight shift with one of the C.P.D. officers. It was a hot and muggy night and fog was starting to move in the low lying areas . . ."

At about 2:00 a.m., Eddie and the officer stopped at the municipal parking lot behind the old Hammers store. Another patrol car joined them. He continues, *"As we chatted, one of the officers stopped talking and was watching a person emerging from the fog . . . we were curious who it might be at that early hour. The person was obviously carrying something as well. We continued to watch as the figure approached. We soon found it was Freddy. He was carrying a huge watermelon. We yelled at Freddy and asked where he got it, but as Freddy typically does when embarrassed or not wanting to comment on a subject, he simply told us it was his and would make no further comment. He continued past us and up Eagle Bend to his home."*

Eddy points out that the area has changed considerably since that night. There were several homes with large gardens that would eventually be replaced by car dealerships. He admits that he has no proof of where that melon came from, but he does conclude, *"When I drove by those gardens the next day, there were some ripe and beautiful melons lying in the sun."*

Even though there may have been a great watermelon heist in progress, the police didn't feel a need to investigate the caper. Instead, Eddie just speaks fondly of how much fun Freddy is to be around.

When Freddy was about twenty-five, he joined some eleven and twelve year olds in a dangerous game of chicken. The agile boys were playing on the railroad tracks, running back and forth as a train approached. Freddy couldn't run back and forth, but he could wait until the last second before jumping off. Someone called the police. The police put everyone in the squad car and made a personal delivery to each parent. Once again, the cops were the protectors.

When it comes to having fun with Freddy, few people enjoy his friendship (and the accompanying teasing) like long time friends Dave Queener and Archie Brummett.

Dave is Steve Queener's brother. Like his brother, he continues his long history of involvement with the Anderson County Fair. And after thirty-three years in the Clinton Police Department, he knows Freddy. So does Archie, who is the Chief of Clinton's Fire Department. Both are Clinton High School graduates. Both are close in age to Freddy. Both love to tease him.

Dave is not a One Bullet Barney. He has been, is, and apparently always be, "Cop." "Cop" began as a patrolman, eventually becoming a detective. He has done his share of midnight shifts, which means he has given Freddy countless rides home in his police car. Freddy was a frequent visitor when Cop was working at the station.

Archie has had his share of visits as well. His name is pronounced, "Arkley." Once, while Freddy was visiting, Arkley took a phone call and proceeded to make up a reported fire. First he said, "At the Towers." He had his visitor's attention. Then he mentioned Freddy's room number. Freddy was out the door before he could tell him he was joking.

Cop and Arkley used to watch Archie's daughter, Destiny, play basketball at Clinton Middle School. This was during the time when half time was Freddy's time. On one occasion, the partners decided it would be fun to perch in the upper balcony of the gym, as obscured as possible, and boo Freddy as he shot. Initially, it was funny – until Freddy started hurling invectives at the boo birds. The pranksters admit – he got the last laugh as they tried to slink away. They may have received a special salute from Freddy.

Dave laughs about a particular Freddyism of days gone by. This particular habit involved drinking a Coke as fast as he could – i.e. killing it. In fact, his exact words were, "I can kill it." If he got a second one, he'd kill that one, too. Dave often wondered if someone kept buying if he would keep killing. Of course, after the killing spree had ended, there was a predictable outcome – besides the obvious bathroom requirement. Invariably, Freddy would grab his stomach and groan, "Ooohh . . . me sick."

Dave is one more member of the law enforcement establishment who has contributed to Freddy's collection of, "Cop equipment," although one contribution was not appreciated. The unappreciative person was an assistant police chief, who did not see the humor in Freddy getting a police shirt (minus the patches) and a night stick. When the assistant chief "reclaimed" those items, Freddy got so mad he stormed into a stand of bushes and refused to come out. Dave had to promise six of Freddy's favorite soft drinks to get him to leave the bushes.

Freddy's "radar" puts him on the scene of so many events. He does not listen to a scanner, but he is often "on the scene" of official police or fire department business. Archie has seen him "assist" in directing traffic at fire drills and real events. Dave has seen him do the same at traffic accidents. Somehow, it all makes sense.

When the Queener/Brummett combo are together, the teasing does not stop. Some of their richest moments include telling Freddy that:

- The rules have changed and he must now pay to attend Clinton High School events.
- He was fired from the pool and could no longer be a lifeguard.
- He was not allowed to direct the band any more.
- And, since Freddy does think of himself as a cop, they've told him he was fired from that job as well.

Yet all the teasing in the world does not change the affection that obviously exists between the three of them. When Dave recently retired from his "day job," Freddy was mad. He wanted his pal to stay on the job forever. Change is not one of his favorite items.

When Archie became a grandfather, Freddy had the typically endearing name for his grandson – Baby Arkley. It's not unusual. Archie's friend Eddy Golden was nicknamed Goose. His younger brother, Johnny had to, under the dictates of Fred logic, be "Baby Goose." Of course Goose was pronounced Goosh.

Dave hosts a sports show on the local access T.V. channel. The show, *Friday Night Scoreboard*, has received calls from Mr. Fagan, especially if his Dragons have won. He likes to call his pal. He also likes to be on T.V.

Dave no longer has a patrol car. He can't drive up behind Freddy and blast the siren. Actually, he wouldn't do that now, not with Freddy's shaky balance, but there was a time when he did. Freddy gave him the same double finger salute he used on Jody Wright when his honking horn made Freddy spill his drinks. Now, Cop and Arkley are left to plot new ways to show their affection.

One plot involves telling Freddy that the book about him has been cancelled – that the author wants to write about Cop and Arkley instead. The other plot involves his street sign.

When Freddy Fagan Way was dedicated, there were two signs made – the one that sits on the pole and identifies his street, and a second one that serves as a back up should something happen to the first. Guess who has access to that sign? Guess which two Clintonites are waiting for just the right time to drive by Freddy and show him the second sign is in their possession – making him think they actually took his street sign.

Once again, the teasing is the ultimate sign of affection. They have grown up together. They care about each other. When Joe Fagan was worried that his brother might be hanging around with people who did not have Freddy's best interests in mind, he asked Officer Queener to talk to him, "Because he'll listen to you." Dave was happy to do so.

He is also happy and proud to point out that, no matter how much he and Archie tease Freddy, when they leave each other, it is important to Freddy that their friendship is solid. Invariably, he will part with, "You me pals," as if to verify that fact. Not that it needs any verification.

And then there is retired Officer Wally Carmichael. He is a member of the elite team of button pushers; in fact, his very presence can cause Freddy to twitch and shake and evoke higher powers to address this bane of his existence.

Wally may very well be the original One Bullet Barney. He got under Freddy's skin early on. Back when Freddy was riding his bike at Jaycee Park, Wally pulled him over and made it clear that he was going to give him a ticket for speeding. When Freddy complained, he threatened to confiscate the bike. "Nos" and "damns" and "bulls" rained down, and even though no tickets were written and no bike was confiscated, the dynamic had been set. In fact, when the "encounter" was over, Freddy went directly to Dave Queener to complain. The words Dave remembers are, "Me no speed." Freddy was appealing to and/or complaining about another cop. Either way, life with Freddy and Wally would get interesting.

Like Dave Queener, Wally would drive his patrol car up to Freddy and blast the horn or the siren. He would do the unthinkable – he would hide Freddy's keys. Few things are more sacred than the keys – and few things would make Freddy madder. Sometimes, Wally was able to distract Freddy enough to sneak the keys back into Freddy's pocket. Then a shocked Freddy would say, "You no got 'em," and Wally could pretend to be mad at Freddy for accusing him of taking his keys.

Wally's personal wealth would be greatly enhanced if he had a dollar for every time he heard, "Damn you Barney." He heard it when he took his shirts and said they were his, when he teased him about wearing girls' clothing, or when he teased him about a classic Freddy moment only he witnessed.

It happened on Main Street. Freddy was walking by the courthouse, a Coke in his strong hand, his keys in the other. He was wearing a pair of loose fitting pants. They kept falling, and Freddy kept trying to hike them up, but his hands were full, and finally gravity won. Freddy's pants fell around his ankles, leaving him standing in his underwear. Freddy set his drink and keys down, hitched up his pants, looked to see if anyone noticed, and went on his way. He did not know that Barney saw it, not until Barney caught up with him and asked, "Did you drop something?" Freddy had to admit that he did, adding, "No belt."

Wally admits to calling Freddy during a basketball game while Freddy was trying to drink a soft drink. He was on the other side of the gym, and timed his call so that Freddy's phone would ring just as he raised the cup to his lips. This would surprise and aggravate the victim, and sometimes cause him to spill his drink, which might seem cruel at first glance, but really isn't. Like Dennis Pratt, and Dave Queener, and Archie Brummett, Wally knows that Freddy thrives on the teasing, that it is actually a sign of affection and a way of making Freddy feel like "one of the guys."

Wally is a C.H.S. graduate. He spent five years as the School Resource Officer (S.R.O.) at his alma mater. He is quick to point out that the main reason for the teasing is just to see Freddy laugh, which he usually does after he gets over being mad.

Once, Wally and his wife, Dale, were at Myrtle Beach when the phone rang. It was Freddy, and Wally greeted him with, "What do you want, Chewie?"

Freddy responded with, "Damn you Barney." Some phone calls are more touching than others.

Wally recently retired from police work. One of his two daughters, Amanda, had a grueling battle with cancer. After the chemo and the hair loss and the pain, she is on her way to a full recovery. It was a harrowing time for the family. During that time, Wally didn't see Freddy. When they finally did see each other, a puzzled Freddy looked at his out of uniform nemesis and asked, "No badge?"

Wally told him he retired, and when he wasn't sure if Freddy understood, he said, "I quit."

That admission caused Freddy to ask a question for the ages: "You no Barney?"

Wally could only laugh and assure him, "You can still call me that if you want to."

When the discussion turned to the fact that Wally hadn't been around lately, Wally explained that Amanda had been very sick. On the verge of tears, Freddy asked, "Your girl sick?" Wally adds, "He really did look like he was going to cry until I told him she was better now."

Freddy has an amazingly tender side – even for those who love to tease him.

Kenny Campbell is the current S.R.O. at Clinton High School, and he has the last word on Freddy and his adventures with the police.

There is a policeman who is, in the modern vernacular, "vertically challenged." The fact that a cop can be short tickles Freddy -- and he is not shy about letting people know, including that officer.

One day, Officer Campbell, the short officer, and two other cops were outside talking when Freddy arrived on the scene. With his usual flair, Freddy began. "Oh God -- all Barneys." Then, as if to amplify his theme, he felt a need to point at each one and establish his individual Barneyness. He pointed at the first and said, "Barney," he pointed at Kenny and said, "Barney," he pointed to the short officer and said, "Half Barney," then he pointed to the final one and said, "Barney."

He dishes it out. He gets it back. In the process, he has built a rare and touching relationship with those in uniform. They are major players in his love story.

No Barney

It is rare that Freddy is rendered speechless. Usually, he is the one doing the rendering. Joe was there when the roles were reversed – in fact, most of the family was, and it is a classic example of things not being what they seem.

Barbara was turning 60. Her friends and relatives conspired to create a memorable birthday party. They decided that they should hire a dancer – a special dancer – an unusual, more exotic type of dancer.

The party was underway when a man in a policeman's uniform knocked on the door. Freddy was probably surprised to see a "cop" he didn't know, but he was undoubtedly happy to have one of his friends in uniform in attendance. At least, he was until the officer asked to speak to Barbara. He began a contrived confrontation, purposely accusing and hassling her about untrue things. Freddy grew uneasy. He may not have understood the particulars, but he certainly sensed something was wrong. Ever the peacemaker, Mr. Ambassador tried to calm things down. According to Joe, he kept telling the officer, "You me pals. It's o.k. – you me pals." That's when the cop gave a signal. The music started and the tear-away cop outfit went flying off – leaving the patrolman in his underwear.

More than a decade later, Joe can't contain his laughter as he says, "You had to see the look on his face. His eyes just got wider and wider." Freddy continued to stare at the now dancing and gyrating "cop," his mouth wide open. He literally was speechless, at least momentarily. Of course, it was only a temporary condition. He recovered. He grabbed Joe's arm tightly and exclaimed, "God damn, Joe! My pal, NO!!"

There are some behaviors that One Bullet Barneys just should not engage in. Freddy was not okay with the Dancing Barney – even after he realized he wasn't a Barney at all.

If only this had become a You Tube sensation. It is also too bad that the unknown dancer wasn't available to give his version of the event. Still, it is easy to imagine and to visualize Freddy and the Dancing Barney. Maybe that should be a permanent feature on the Don Calhoun/Alvin Taylor T.V. show.

The Shark

It is 2011. The regular season is over, and tournament action has begun for the C.H.S. baseball team. The Dragons play in the first game, and they win. The entire coaching staff, including Freddy, stays to watch Oak Ridge play in the second game. The Pussycats would also win.

At the conclusion of the second game, a familiar scene plays out on the field. The teams form two lines, exchange handshakes, and gradually collect their equipment and leave. Well-wishers trickle onto the field to congratulate or commiserate with the winning and losing players and coaches. The Clinton staff is part of the scene.

As intense as the Oak Ridge rivalry can be, as much as the respective coaches enjoy beating the other, there is a healthy respect that exists between them, so it was not unusual for Casey and Alvin and Freddy to offer congratulations to Coach Froning. They did so as Tom's three daughters approached to celebrate with their dad. At the time, the girls were ten, eight, and five years old.

Freddy saw the three girls and made the connection – they were Pussycat Coach's girls. As if to verify that, he pointed at Tom, then his girls, and held up three fingers. It was a non-verbal exercise, and Tom responded, "Yes, Freddy, those are my three girls."

Freddy then put his hands together and slowly raised the top hand as a way to indicate growth. Once again, Tom played the interpreter. "You are right Freddy, they are growing up." That remark led Freddy to look at the girls, then their father. He assessed the situation and succinctly gave his verdict with the words, "You broke!"

Where does that kind of thought process originate? What leads to that kind of hilarious conclusion? Of course, most parents of growing siblings would concur, but how does Freddy know about such issues?

Eventually, the Dragons would lose in tournament play. That would leave only one item left on the baseball agenda. That would be the team banquet. The banquet was held at the site of an old car dealership that was converted to a new entertainment center. It is a hall that can be rented for any number of occasions, including dances, and parties, and banquets. It is close to the school and big enough to accommodate large gatherings.

High school baseball in the state of Tennessee ends in May – the month of Freddy's birth. So a parent baked a cake for the birthday boy. The facility had room for the teammates to play pool and ping pong. Guess who became a prime time player in the game room?

Table tennis is not his forte. The type of eye/hand coordination required is especially challenging. He had trouble with the serve, and his return of serve was an adventure. Casey found a baseball analogy for it. He said it was like watching Cecil Fielder hit. It was often all or nothing – a strike out or a home run. Freddy whiffed often, but he hit his share of homers, and if that isn't exactly the purpose of the game, he didn't care, nor did anyone else.

Pool is a different story. The balls are stationary, and Freddy had a long history of visiting local pool halls when he was younger, so he does reasonably well. In Freddy's mind, he is a real hustler, and his "hustle" would lead to another classic comment.

Freddy was trying to tell Casey how good he was. He kept saying, "Me pool . . . something." Casey couldn't figure out what he was saying to him, but it sounded like, "Me pool shot." Casey replied, "I see, you're going to make a pool shot."

"No Cray Cray. Me pool . . . something." Casey needed relief help, so he called to the bullpen for the master interpreter. Alvin came, heard what Freddy was saying, and as only he can do, immediately discerned, "He's telling you he is a pool shark."

Of course. Freddy The Pool Shark. He would repeat the phrase often. Like his assessment of Tom Froning and his growing daughters, (i.e. – "You broke") one has to wonder, where did he learn it? Why did it stick with him? How was he able to remember it at such an appropriate time?

Five years earlier, at the celebration of his 50th birthday, he was reluctant to share his birthday cake. At the banquet, he was willing to do so. "Boys cake" was his offer. He knows he has to be careful, that too much cake and, "Me sick."

Another season ends. Another banquet is held, with Freddy being an integral part of the festivities. There would be summer league games to go to, and the count down to football season would begin. The players and coaches would be left with the memories that high school athletics consistently etches into the minds of the participants. Over time, the members of the 2011 team will realize what decades of C.H.S. athletes have come to understand; that in time, many of their fondest memories will include Mr. Fagan.

For Casey Taylor, the single most vivid baseball memory of 2011 did not take place on the field. It occurred on the way to a game at Halls High School in Knoxville. Casey was driving his car. Freddy was his passenger. The other coaches and players were following on the team bus. They were almost at their destination, in fact the school was in sight, but they were stuck in traffic. Freddy's leg was bouncing up and down, and the coach knew that was not a good sign. No cars were moving when Casey asked Freddy if he had to use the bathroom. Freddy told him yes. Casey pointed to the school and asked if he thought he could make it. He heard, "No Cray Cray. Me gotta go now." The road had no shoulder to speak of. Casey maneuvered as far off the road as he could, and Freddy went as far from the car as he could get, but considering they were basically in city traffic, Freddy was not far from the road when he found relief. Of course, by the time Freddy got situated, the light had changed, the traffic got unsnarled, and the team bus came rolling by. That's when the hooting and catcalls and teasing started. Freddy would answer the teasers.

For the Taylors, there is more to coaching than strategy and batting order and personnel moves. Issues like transportation and bladder control are equally important. For as long as he lives, Casey will remember Freddy and the team bus and a busy Knoxville intersection. It is one more memory, one more story, one more classic adventure in the travels with a pool shark. Who can ask for more?

The Contradictions

Freddy is a mass of contradictions. He is simple, yet complex – inarticulate, yet eloquent – shy yet gregarious. He is man child – in fact, he is an old man/child.

He has the bladder control and medicinal regimen of the elderly. He is dependent on routine and ritual and habit, yet he is perpetually young. He still believes in Santa Claus. In 2010, Jeff Kidwell took an excited Freddy to have his picture taken with Santa. His unbridled excitement for any big event in Clinton is the epitome of childlike innocence.

He is naïve enough that he can be a target, an easy victim for the unscrupulous, yet he is a hustler, a con man in his own right. Clinton City Manager Roger Houck has seen the hustler in action. His first encounter was in 1987, when Roger was the director of the city's Park and Recreation Department. Having grown up in Lake City, he knew of Freddy, but it wasn't until they met at the Clinton Community Center that he got the full treatment.

It was Halloween. Freddy was "working." He was going around the center with a big bag, saying "Trick Treat." Apparently the "or" just got in the way. When he got to Mr. Houck, he opened the bag, waiting for a deposit. Roger explains, "I looked down, expecting to see candy. There was not one piece of candy in the bag. It was full of bills, and they weren't one dollar bills, either." He laughs as he adds, "It's hard not to contribute in a situation like that."

Of course, Freddy would continue the "shakedown" at the

courthouse and numerous other establishments, and it wasn't just at Halloween. Birthdays and Christmas provided great opportunities for citizens to contribute. And some people give him money just because . . . because it is 2:00 on a Tuesday, or three days before the fair, summer solstice eve, or the Sunday after the Vols' first football game. Somehow he gets all this money, and yet he is not a beggar, or intrusive, or inappropriate. It is part of his charm.

He is dependent on the kindness of others, yet fiercely independent, especially if he feels confined.

He doesn't know math, and he certainly doesn't know fractions, but somehow he can calculate a half-Barney. He can't do simple arithmetic, but he manages to use a cell phone, and he has figured out that twenty dollars is better than five, and that five dollars beats, "one damn dollar" any day.

He can't tell time, but he is never late for a big event or a, "Ball game, ball game." Many in Clinton have marveled at his "radar," his innate ability to be where the action is, to suddenly, magically appear.

If a woman appears during boy talk, he becomes quiet. Mention his trips to Hooters around certain family members or his girlfriends and he will appear to be shyest man on the planet. He may hold a finger to his lips to shush the offending betrayer of secrets. He may even blush. Give him a microphone and he becomes an uninhibited Elvis. Take him to a wrestling match and he is wilder than the wrestlers.

At times, no one is tackier. His brother John provides an example of that. Freddy has a shirt that has a certain "Christmas scene" on it. That scene has also been used on tacky Christmas cards. It features Santa and his sleigh, and they have stopped in front of an outhouse. The caption reads, "No Rudolph, I said the *Schmidt* house." John doesn't know where he got the shirt. He does know that it was Freddy's choice to wear to church one Sunday. Not that he was purposely being tacky – he did not totally appreciate the inappropriateness of it. Sometimes things happen. If a man has 1,200 shirts, there are bound to be some that aren't church-wear.

Sometimes Freddy is tacky when he is trying to be virtuous. That was shown during a period when Freddy was a regular at church. He loved the hymns and the fellowship and the entire experience. He wanted to make sure others were also experiencing that feeling. Unfortunately, Freddy doesn't always "filter" things. He sometimes mixes the religious use of the word God with his propensity to cuss. He actually cusses far less now than he used to, but about a decade ago, after attending church, he felt the need to share his feeling with his pal Alvin.

He called Coach. He told Coach he had been to church. Things were fine. Then he asked Coach if he had gone to church. Alvin was forced to admit that, on that particular Sunday, he had, in fact, not attended church. Freddy responded, "Ooohh . . . God damn God gonna get you!"

It is hard to know exactly how to respond to such a warning. It was vintage Freddy. He was sincere and concerned and trying to help his friend. If anyone else said it, it would be considered offensive, perhaps sacrilegious. But for all of the tackiness, there is a simple yet eloquent message from Father Fagan, no matter how he phrased it.

The contradictions that surround Freddy only help to make him more interesting, and the final contradiction may be the most interesting of all. For the most part, he is amazingly consistent. He can often be counted on to say or do certain things in certain situations. There is a litany of expressions and behaviors for ball games, birthdays, and the fair. Yet it is also true that no one ever really knows what he will say or do next. That's the fun part of the Freddy Experience. It is what makes him unique. There will never be another one like him.

And In the End . . .

Freddy's story does not end. It can't. As long as he is active and healthy, there will be new encounters and adventures – new classic moments for people to share. And when he is no longer active and healthy, his story will continue, because the children and the grandchildren of Clinton know his story, and they will tell their children and grandchildren. Like his street sign, Freddy's story will endure. There is permanence in his legacy.

Freddy's story is a love story; a love story of the highest magnitude. No one loves his town more than he does. No one is more beloved by his town than he is.

Once upon a time, a child was born in Germany. He was born with physical and mental challenges. He would move to several different places before luck, or fate, or divine intervention, or some cosmic force in the universe determined that his family would plant their roots in Clinton, Tennessee. The consequences of that one single act would alter countless lives.

As in all good love stories, there would be obstacles to overcome. There would be conflict and antagonists and outrageous fortunes. He would suffer the slings of stigma, the arrows of prejudice and ignorance. He would be physically beaten and verbally abused by the villains who always try to alter the course of a love story. Those villains would fail. Those villains always fail.

In 1996, then First Lady Hillary Clinton published a book titled *It Takes a Village.* The title comes from an African proverb that suggests there are many people outside of the family who contribute to the growth of a child.

If Mrs. Clinton wished to see the ultimate practice of her book's theory, she should come to Anderson County. She should see what the "village" of Clinton has done to raise Freddy Fagan. There are myriad villagers who have nurtured and guided and loved him. They have fed him and bathed him and clothed him. In the process, the villagers have become kinder, gentler people.

The Fagan family is acutely aware of just how special this love story is. Every one of them has expressed their gratitude to the town that has enabled a special needs child to grow up to be called mayor, ambassador, and king. They know that there are many places where this does not happen. They know that the way Clinton has embraced Freddy is uniquely special.

Freddy's story does not end, but books do. This one ends with one more classic Freddy moment. Fittingly, it is a moment on a bus – a bus taking the baseball team to a game in Oak Ridge. Alvin and Freddy are seated in the front. This time they aren't engaged in boy talk. This time it is man talk.

It is 2004 – shortly after Freddy's father passed away from esophageal cancer. As the bus passed the Holley Gamble Funeral Home, Freddy's thoughts were on death and mortality. Ever the philosopher, he broached the topic of what would happen when they died. Using his unique way of saying the word die, he asked, "You guy?"

Alvin responded, "Yes, when I die, what?"

"You guy, me keys."

"You're going to take my keys when I die?"

Freddy assured him that he was, indeed, interested in his keys. The subject of Freddy's death produced a much different reaction. It provides a stunning insight into Freddy's knowledge of his place in the community. In response to Alvin's question, with no hesitation, Freddy responded, "Me guy? Downtown . . . Close. . . School . . . Out."

Downtown close. School out. In four words, Freddy captured the essence of his stature. When the people of Clinton hear this story, virtually every person has the same two thoughts. The order may vary, and the phrasing may change, but the main ideas do not change.

One immediate reaction can be summed up in three words: "He is right." It is universally understood that the final celebration of his life will be the biggest such celebration in the town's history.

The other immediate reaction takes the form of a hope, wish, prayer, plea or some combination of all of those. It can be expressed with the words, "Not any time soon." No one wants to think about that. Instead, they wish to focus on the continuing saga that is Freddy's story.

There are ball games to attend and girlfriends to visit. There are future trips to Hooters and more days at the Anderson County Fair. There are umps and refs to hassle and a band to lead. There are hearts to touch and a town to run. That's just the way it is when you are the central figure in a love story.